The Royle Family

The Royle Family

The Scripts: Series 2

Caroline Aherne, Craig Cash
and Carmel Morgan

GRANADA

First published in Great Britain in 2000
by Granada Media, an imprint of André Deutsch Ltd
in association with Granada Media Group
76 Dean Street
London W1V 5HA
www.vci.co.uk

The Royle Family is a Granada Television Production

A catalogue record for this book is available
from the British Library

ISBN 0 233 99901 9

Plate section design by Design 23

Typeset by Derek Doyle & Associates, Liverpool
Printed and bound in Great Britain by
Mackays of Chatham plc, Chatham, Kent

Cover designed by
Leslie Barbazette

Photographs reproduced courtesy of
Granada Media, except for pictures on
final page of plate section, © BBC

Contents

Acknowledgements

We would like to thank our brilliant cast:

Geoffrey Hughes, Sue Johnston, Doreen Keogh, Ralf Little, Peter Martin, Liz Smith, Sheridan Smith, Jessica Stevenson, Ricky Tomlinson and Andrew Whyment.

And crew:

Nick Adams, Guy Barker, David Barrett, Paula Barrington-Rossiter, Paul Beeson, Terry Black, Grace Boylan, Peter Bremner, Christine Cant, Billy Charlton, Caroline Coleman, Gordon Craig, Tony Cranstoun, James Dillon, Jimmy Dyson, Sheena Gunn, Peter Hallam, Annie Hardinge, Belinda Harris, Diane Kasperowicz, Edward Knight, Samuel Leek, Tony Lenman, Susie Liddell, Sandy MacRae, Kamala Maniam, Paul Michel, John Miles, Chrissie Moses, Jan Murphy, Mel Northcliffe, Mike Popley, Dave Radcliffe, Mike Reardon, Simon Reglar, Sara Reisal, John Rushton, Alexander Sahla, David Sanderson, Martin Shepherd, Andy Stagles, Ben Webster, June West, Helen Williams, John Wood, Phil Wood.

We would also like to thank the following:

Kenton Allen, Lucy Ansbro, Steve Bendelack, Ealing Studios, Granada Television, Andy Harries, Bruce Lloyd, Danielle Lucks, Phil McIntyre, Patti Marr, Paul Roberts, Peter Salmon, Matt Squire, Brian Viner – and all at Creation Records.

Introduction

Introduction, my arse!

Love

Caroline Aherne and Craig Cash

(*A small drinking club, Soho, July 2000*)

Cast list

DENISE ROYLE	CAROLINE AHERNE
DAVE BEST	CRAIG CASH
TWIGGY	GEOFFREY HUGHES
BARBARA ROYLE (MAM)	SUE JOHNSTON
MARY CARROLL	DOREEN KEOGH
ANTONY ROYLE	RALF LITTLE
JOE CARROLL	PETER MARTIN
NORMA SPEAKMAN (NANA)	LIZ SMITH
EMMA	SHERIDAN SMITH
CHERYL CARROLL	JESSICA STEVENSON
JIM ROYLE (DAD)	RICKY TOMLINSON
DARREN	ANDREW WHYMENT

Episode 1

LIVING ROOM

JIM, BARBARA AND ANTONY ALL WATCHING TV

Barbara: Don't it look lovely there.

Jim: Bermuda my arse.

Barbara: She's looking her age though in't she, Judith Chalmers.

Jim: I don't know. How old is she?

Barbara: I don't know.

JIM LOOKS AT BARBARA. PAUSE.

Barbara: She's got some lovely wrap-round skirts though. Who do you think's the oldest, her or Gloria Hunniford, Jim? Jim?

Jim: What?

Barbara: Who do you think's the eldest, her or Gloria Hunniford?

Jim: I couldn't give a shiny shite. Bloody 'ell, Barb.

BARBARA SHAKES HER HEAD. PAUSE.

Antony: Eh, y'know Darren's cousin, Steve?

Barbara: Yeah.

Antony: He's been abroad twice this year.

Barbara: Ooh.

Jim: Oh aye, where did he go to, lad?

Antony: Ah, he went to Magaluf in February and, eh, Lloret de Mar in July.

Jim: He's hardly Alan bloody, Whicker is he? Na, them foreign holidays are a swizz. Them bloody travel agents ripping every bugger off and mugs like him fall for it.

Barbara: What they falling for, Jim?

Jim: Well, there's nothing you can do abroad that you can't do here. It just costs you twice as bloody much.

Barbara: They're on their holidays – they're having a good time.

Jim: Having a good time, my arse. They spend half the time on the khazi, don't they, having the wild shites. You may as well do that here in the comfort of your own home.

Barbara: You are a miserable sod, Jim, you are.

PAUSE. ANTONY LAUGHS.

DOORBELL RINGS.

Jim: Get that door will ya, Antony, and if it's the invisible man, tell him, I can't see him. (LAUGHS) The invisible man.

DENISE AND DAVE ARE AT THE LIVING ROOM DOOR.

Denise: Hi ya.

Antony: It's all right, it's only Dave and Denise.

DENISE AND DAVE ENTER. THEY ALL SAY 'HI YA'. THEY SIT DOWN.

Jim: Y'all right, Dave?

Barbara: Y'all right, love?

Denise: Yeah.

Barbara: You all right, Dave?

Dave: Yeah.

Barbara: Aah.

THEY ALL WATCH TELLY.

Barbara: Have you had your teas?

Denise/Dave: Yeah.

PAUSE.

Barbara: Aah. What d'ya have?

Denise: Dairylea on toast.

Jim: Bloody 'ell, I bet you were looking forward to that all day, eh, Dave? Woo. Working hard, waiting to get home to that little delicacy.

Denise: Shut it, Dad.

Jim: Bloody 'ell girl, Dairylea on toast. Come on now. Eh? Delia Smith's got nothing to worry about, has she.

Denise: I made it meself.

Dad: Go 'way.

Dave: I don't mind Dairylea, me.

PAUSE.

Barbara: Can I make you a nice bacon butty, Dave?

Dave: Oh yeah, please Barbara, that'd be lovely.

DAVE CATCHES DENISE'S EYE.

Barbara: Go and put some bacon on for us will ya, Antony.

ANTONY GOES TO KITCHEN.

Denise: (TO DAVE) You're making a right show of me, Dave. You said that was enough for ya.

Dave: It's only a bit of bacon.

Jim: Aye, a bit of my bloody bacon.

Denise: Oh Antony, put some under for me 'n' all.

CUT TO JIM'S FACE. PAUSE. ALL CONTINUE TO WATCH TELLY.

Denise: Dad.

Dad: What?

Denise: Your fly-hole's all undone.

Jim: (ZIPPING IT UP) Ah, the cage might be open but the beast is asleep.

Barbara: Beast my arse.

CUT TO JIM'S FACE. PAUSE. ALL CONTINUE TO WATCH TELLY.

PAUSE.

Denise: Mam.

Barbara: Umm.

Denise: Mam, can you ask our Antony to make my bacon dead, dead crispy.

Barbara: Yeah, Antony, can you make Denise's bacon dead, dead crispy.

PAUSE. ALL WATCHING TV. BARBARA LIGHTS UP.

Barbara: (OFFERING CIGGY) 'Ere y'are love.

Denise: Oh, no thanks.

JIM AND BARBARA LOOK OVER AT DENISE.

Barbara: What's up with yer?

Denise: Nothing.

Barbara: Have you given up?

Denise: Yeah.

Barbara: You've always loved smoking.

Denise: Yeah well, me and Dave's got something to tell ya.

Dave: You said you weren't gonna-say owt?

Denise: Yeah, I know, well, I am now.

Dave: You said it was a big secret.

Denise: Yeah, but that was this morning. Mam, Dad, we're pregnant.

Jim: Bloody 'ell. Put it there, David. Well done. Well done, lad.

Dave: Thanks, James.

Jim: Come here my little glow-worm. Well done. Well done, love.

Barbara: Oh, I can't believe it. I can't believe it.

JIM STANDS UP, GOES OVER TO DENISE ON THE SETTEE AND GIVES HER A KISS.

Barbara: (CALLS OUT TO KITCHEN) Oh, er, Antony, our Denise and Dave are having a baby.

Antony: (STICKS HEAD ROUND DOOR) Oh, nice one.

Jim: Put a bit of bacon under for the baby will ya, lad.

Denise: I can't believe our Antony, there's a new life forming in my womb. He's not even arsed.

Barbara: Ooh, God, Denise. Ooh, I'll have to have a ciggy. When's it due?

Denise: In January.

Barbara: January. Oh, are you pleased, Dave?

Dave: Yeah. Delighted.

Jim: Well, they don't come cheap you know, son. You'll have to get stuck in there now, get in all the overtime you can. (TO DENISE) Well done, Denise. Eh, at least you can do something bloody properly.

Barbara: I can't believe it. I can't believe it. I can't.

Denise: Can you believe it?

Barbara: Yeah.

BARBARA BLOWS SMOKE ON DENISE AND WAVES IT AWAY.

Denise: Oh no, no I like it. Ooh, lovely. Aah, Mam. Aah. Aah, Mam. Aah, Dave, look at me mam.

Dave: I know.

Denise: Aah.

Barbara: Do you know, I've been waiting for this day all my life.

Denise/Dave: (TOGETHER) Aah.

Barbara: I can't tell you how happy you've made me.

Denise: Aah.

Barbara: Are your mam and dad pleased, Dave?

Dave: Well, I've not really told them yet, Barbara, you know with it being a secret 'n' all.

Barbara: Oh, yeah. Ah, Jim, our first grandchild.

Jim: I know, I can't bloody believe it.

Barbara: When did you find out?

Denise: Well, me period was late, right, (JIM SHOOTS A LOOK OF DISDAIN) and then I was really really sick, but I thought, oh, you know, it was just a hangover 'cause the night before we'd had a lock-in at the Feathers. But then the next day, I was really sick again so I went down Boots, right, and got a pregnancy kit – ten quid they are – and, 'em anyway, the line came up in the square window.

Barbara: (REALLY EXCITED) Oh, Denise – the square window.

Denise: Yes. So I was shouting for Dave at the top of the stairs – but he was watching something on telly. What was you watching, Dave?

Dave: *Never Mind the Buzzcocks.*

Denise: And 'em, then he come up. And I'm like this: 'Hey Daddy, Daddy, guess what?', like that to him, didn't I, Dave?

Dave: Ummm.

Barbara: And did he know what you meant?

Denise/Dave: (TOGETHER) No, no.

Denise: But then I said, you know, 'Dave, I'm pregnant', like that and, er, the penny dropped, didn't it?

Dave: Yeah, straight away, yeah.

Denise: And eh, then I let him have a little look in the square window.

Barbara: Ooh, the square window. Bet you were delighted weren't you, Dave?

Dave: Oh yeah. Big style.

Jim: Ten pounds for a bloody pregnancy test. Bloody highway robbery.

Barbara: Our Denise. God.

PAUSE. ALL WATCH TELLY.

BARBARA AND DENISE CONTINUE TO EXCHANGE LOOKS OF DELIGHT AND DISBELIEF. JIM LOOKS WISTFUL.

Denise: Ah, do you know, last night, right, we was watching *Animal Hospital* and Dave had his head there on me belly and he was just talking to the baby.

Barbara: Aah.

Jim: Knobhead.

Barbara: What do you want, Dave?

Dave: A boy. Yeah.

Denise: Or a girl.

Dave: Or a girl, yeah. Or a girl.

Barbara: Aaah.

PAUSE.

Barbara: Antony. Bring me the phone. (ANTONY GOES TO HALL TO GET PHONE) I'm gonna tell your nana.

Denise: Aah. Mam, will you let me tell her?

Barbara: Oh, all right then. (DIALS DELIGHTEDLY ON PHONE) Hiya, hiya, Mam. Mam, our Denise and Dave have got something very special to tell you. (PAUSE) Oh, okay then. Bye. (PUTS PHONE DOWN) Can we ring her back after Corrie.

Jim: I wouldn't ring her back for bloody spite now. Bloody old snatch.

Barbara: Jim.

Jim: Well . . .

Denise: Dave's making a start on making that box-room into a nursery.

Barbara: Aah.

Jim: Well, what are you gonna do with the moped that was in it?

Denise: Ey, that's going.

Dave: That's going nowhere.

Barbara: Dave, you can't put a newborn baby in with a moped.

Dave: I'll put a cover on it.

ANTONY RETURNS AND HANDS OUT THE BUTTIES.

Antony: Hey, it's great news that, our kid. I can't wait.

Denise: Aah.

Barbara: Well, give your sister a kiss. Shake Dave's hand. Where's your manners?

Antony: Nice one, Dave.

Dave: Cheers, Antony.

Denise: Aah. (PAUSE) Antony, where's the red sauce for Dave.

Dave: No red sauce.

Jim: Get the red sauce you lazy sod. God, he's bone idle. Don't know where he gets it from.

ANTONY TUTS AND GOES BACK TO KITCHEN.

Barbara: Eh, Denise, you're eating for two now.

Denise: Ooh, yeah. Aah, in't it lovely.

Barbara: Yeah.

Denise: Do you know what? I really, really hope it's a girl.

Barbara: Ooh, yeah.

Denise: I'm gonna get her ears pierced you know, before the christening.

Jim: You can get her tattooed as well, while you're at it.

ANTONY RETURNS WITH SAUCE.

Dave: Cheers, buddy.

Denise: Hey, Antony, we've got you down as the main babysitter.

Antony: Kiss my arse.

Jim: Nice one, Lurch.

Barbara: Me and Dad will do all your babysitting you know.

JIM'S REACTION.

Denise: Thanks.

Barbara: Anyway, what am I thinking about? We should be celebrating. Antony, nip down the offy and get us some Pomagne.

Jim: Eh, never mind Pomagne. Nothing but the best for this

baby. (LOOKS IN HIS WALLET) How about the old champagne? Eh, well how much is that going to set me back?

Antony: 'Bout twenty-five quid.

Jim: 'Ere y'are, there's a fiver – just get a bottle of Pomagne. Well,
bloody 'ell, it's not twins, is it?

Antony: Anyway, Denise, you're not supposed to have any.

Denise: Yeah, I am. I mean, I can't get tanked up like most
nights, but I can have a good old couple, can't I, Mam?

Barbara: Oh yeah. I did with you two.

PAUSE. ANTONY GOES TO OFFY.

Barbara: Denise, have you thought about any names yet?

Denise: I've thought about nothing else, but everything I like, he
doesn't like. If it's a girl, I really want Whitney.

Barbara: Aah, Whitney. That's gorgeous. Whitney. What if it's a
boy?

Denise: Well, I really want Keanu, but Dave wants Dave.

Barbara: I don't think you should have a Dave.

Denise: No.

Barbara: I mean, Dave's Dave. What do you think, Jim?

Jim: Eh? What about?

Barbara: Well, if it's a boy, Dave wants to call it Dave.

Jim: (TO DAVE) Well, you're already a Dave. What d'you want
another one for? Come on, son, get a bloody grip of yourself.

Denise: See.

Dave: Well, it's like handing it down, innit. I mean, my dad was Dave, and his dad, and I think his dad was as well. PAUSE. And his dad.

Jim: Well it's about time you put a bloody stop to it. C'mon.

PAUSE.

Barbara: Hey, Denise, isn't it funny, you being pregnant . . . You know Lorraine across the road?

Denise: Leggings Lorraine?

Barbara: Yeah, she's been sterilized.

Denise: Has she?

Barbara: Yeah. Well, four's enough for any single mother.

Jim: I bet it's like a clown's pocket there, eh Dave?

Barbara: Jim.

Jim: What?

Denise: Dave.

Dave: Mmm?

Denise: The baby wants some milk.

Dave: Right.

Jim: (WATCHING DAVE GET UP) Look at the big soft sod.

Denise: Dad! I'm pregnant. I've got to take it easy now.

Jim: What d'you mean, 'now'?

Barbara: Well, she's right, she's got to drink a lot of milk – it's good for the baby's teeth.

Denise: Is it?

Barbara: Ooh yeah.

DAVE RETURNS WITH MILK.

Dave: Here y'are, Mummy.

Denise: Aah. Thanks, Dave.

PAUSE.

Barbara: Denise, have you thought whether you'll breastfeed or not?

Jim: Oh, I wouldn't if I was you, love. That's why the springs have gone in your mother's . . . (MOTIONS SAGGY KNOCKERS)

Barbara: You cheeky sod, Jim. Eh, eh, I haven't got bad boobs for a woman of my age.

Jim: Ooh, behave will you, Barb. They're like bloody spaniel's ears.

Barbara: Oh right. Right, well, that's the last time you see 'em then.

Jim: 'Ey, I'll not put the mockers on your shrivelled knockers.

Denise: No, I'm not gonna breastfeed. Been thinking about it, right, and if the baby wants a feed in the night with my breasts, it'll mean me having to wake up. Well, if it's bottle-fed and everything, Dave can do it, you know, when you're not there? 'Cause I've got to keep my independence, that's the thing.

Barbara: Ooh yeah – yeah, you must keep your independence. Anyway, the bottled stuff's just as good.

Denise: D'you know what size it is now?

Barbara: Ooh no, what size?

Denise: Erm, what was it again, Dave?

Dave: I dunno.

Denise: Oh, what was it? Oh yeah, the size of a little nut.

Barbara: A little nut.

Denise: Yeah.

Barbara: Ah, Denise. A nut. Ah Dave. Eh, Dave, are you gonna be changing the nappies?

Dave: Oh aye, I'm gonna get involved, me.

Barbara: Aah, oh ey, it's all different nowadays.

Denise: Yeah, bet Dad never changed our nappies.

Barbara: Oh, did he hell.

Jim: No, I'm still wiping her arse now twenty-odd years later.

Barbara: Jim.

Jim: Well . . .

Denise: Oh, do you know what Dave's getting? You know one of those things you put there and then you put the baby in it there and then you carry it around.

Jim: Are you Dave? (JIM LAUGHS. DOES LIMP WRIST).

Dave: That's not definite yet, Denise.

Denise: Dave, you said you were.

Dave: Well, I'm not – I'm not – I'm not definite about that yet.

Denise: Dave, I'll have been carrying it around in me belly for nine months all on me own.

Barbara: You can always leave it here you know, when you're shopping.

Jim: 'Leave it here?' It's their bloody baby.

PAUSE.

Denise: We're not gonna be able to have a nanny straight away, you know.

Barbara: Aah.

Jim: What bloody nanny?

Denise: Well I can't look after it full-time. I've got to keep my independence, Dad.

Jim: What bloody independence? Sitting on your arse all day watching Richard and Judy?

Barbara: Well, I think she's right.

Jim: Well, why don't you leave the baby here and just come and visit the bugger once a week.

ANTONY RETURNS WITH POMAGNE.

Antony: Eh, I got some Asti.

THEY ALL CHEER.

Denise: Oh, I love Asti.

Jim: Change please.

Antony: Oh ey, Denise, I saw Duckers and I told him and he was made up about the baby, so.

Denise: What you telling people about the baby for? It's mine and Dave's baby. Mam, will you tell Antony to stop telling everyone?

Barbara: Stop telling everyone, Antony.

Antony: I've only told Duckers.

Denise: Oh, cheers. So Duckers knows about it before me own nana.

Jim: Your own bloody nana's more bloody interested in bloody *Coronation Street* than the baby.

Barbara: Jim. How many bloodies is that? (SHE GETS OUT THE GLASSES) Anyway, c'mon, let's celebrate.

SHE PUTS OUT GLASSES AND JIM OPENS POMAGNE.

Jim: Here we go. Here we go, here we go. Nice one, Barb.

Barbara: Now watch these glasses here. Be very careful with them.

Denise: Loads for me. I'm drinking for two.

Barbara: All right. Right, pass that over please.

Jim: Lots more here please, Barb, for your little husband. Ladies and gentlemen, it gives me great pleasure to be able to say that, er, we know that Dave isn't firing blanks.

ANTONY KILLS HIMSELF LAUGHING. THEY ALL RAISE THEIR GLASSES: 'WAAAY'.

Dave: I'm no jaffa.

Antony: Eh, might not even be Dave's.

Denise: Antony, why do you have to spoil everything? Course it's Dave's.

Barbara: Of course it's Dave's.

Dave: Course it's mine.

Jim: Anyway, right. To David, Denise and little Keanu – all the best.

All: Keanu!

Denise: Or Whitney.

THEY CLINK GLASSES.

All: Or Whitney!

Jim: Ey Denise, I'm made up for you. (TO ANTONY) Ey, don't neck it, Antony.

Antony: Can I have another?

Jim: No you can't. I'm absolutely made up with you being pregnant because, you know, if it was left up to old gay boy over there, we'd never have any grandkids.

Barbara: Ooh, Jim – it's a celebration.

BARBARA LIGHTS UP.

Jim: Oh he's a little old bummer. I'll tell you what, it's worth a few extra bob that, innit?

Barbara: Dave, are you gonna be at the birth?

Dave: Ooh aye. I wouldn't miss that, Barbara.

Barbara: Aah.

Jim: You're not, are you, Dave? Ooh, you're not going at the goal end are you? (HE CLOSES HIS LEGS)

Dave: No.

Barbara: Least he won't be in the pub like you were.

Jim: I couldn't get in between you and your mother on the bloody day.

Denise: You're gonna be there 'n'all, Mam?

Barbara: Ooh yeah.

Denise: I'm gonna ask Cheryl 'n'all.

Jim: Why don't you just put a turnstile in the maternity ward.

PAUSE.

Denise: Oh, I've not even told Cheryl yet. Antony, go and get Cheryl.

Antony: You go and get her.

Denise: I've got to rest – I'm with child.

Jim: Ey, Lurch, go on. Do as your bloody sister asks ya. Where does he get it from, him?

ANTONY EXITS.

Denise: (SHOUTS) Don't you go telling her. I wanna tell her. (PAUSE). Eh, I'm gonna ask Cheryl to be godmother.

Barbara: Are you?

Denise: Yeah.

Barbara: Aah.

Denise: Well, she'll be great, Cheryl.

Barbara: Ooh yeah.

Denise: And if I ask her to be godmother, she'll never mind when I ask her to babysit.

Jim: Why don't you just get the baby adopted, too? Bloody 'ell there's nothing like a mother's love is there?

Barbara: Denise.

Denise: Mmmm?

Barbara: Are you going to ask Antony to be godfather?

Denise: No. Anyway, Dave wants Gary.

Barbara: Oh, do you, Dave?

Dave: Well, his mum died recently Barbara, y'know, and I owe him two hundred quid, y'know, so it should hold him off for a bit, y'know.

Barbara: Oh, yes. Yeah.

PAUSE.

Denise: Mam, where's Antony with Cheryl?

Jim: He'll be a while yet, won't he. He'll still be trying to prise her bloody head out of the fridge. I'm gonna move this anyway, before she spots it.

Denise: He'd better not have said anything.

Barbara: Don't worry, he won't.

WE HEAR SINGING – CLIFF RICHARD'S 'CONGRATULA-TIONS AND CELEBRATIONS . . .', ETC, AS MARY AND CHERYL RUN IN SINGING, FOLLOWED BY JOE (NOT SINGING) WHO LAGS BEHIND.
MARY AND CHERYL KISS DENISE AND DAVE.

Mary: Oh, congratulations.

Denise: Thanks, Mary.

Mary: I'm so pleased for you both. Ooh, Dave!

Dave: Thanks, Mary.

MARY KISSES BARBARA. SHE TURNS TO JIM, DECIDES AGAINST KISSING HIM.

Mary: It's lovely, isn't it; Jim?

Cheryl: I can't believe it now, we were only watching the wedding video again last night. Isn't that weird?

Barbara: Weird.

Jim: All right, Joe? What do you think of the news?

Joe: Oh, aye.

Mary: I knew you were pregnant, Denise, as soon as Antony said it.

Denise: Aah.

Denise: Cheryl, guess who I want to be godmother?

Cheryl: Who?

Denise: You!

Cheryl: Ooh, Denise.

Mary: Oh, sweet Jesus!

Jim: That's just 'cause she'll babysit all the bloody time.

Barbara: Oh, Jim! Take no notice of him, love.

Cheryl: Oh no, I'd love to look after it all the time.

Denise: Aah. Cheers, Cheryl.

Mary: When's it due?

Denise: January.

Cheryl: January. If it's early January it'll be a Capricorn, but if it's later January then it'll be Aquarius.

Denise: Well I'm gonna try and hold on if I can till January 'cause Dave's Aquarius.

Mary: Ooh, are you an Aquarius, Dave?

Dave: Yeah, I am, yeah.

Mary: Joe's Aquarius.

Barbara: Ooh, are you Aquarius, Joe?

Joe: Yeah.

Jim: Let's hope the baby's Capricorn then, eh. Oh ey, Joe, do you want to go to the birth? Our Denise is organizing a coach trip.

PAUSE.

Joe: A little baby, eh? A little baby.

Cheryl: God, I can't believe it – I'm so made up. Denise, you can eat for two now.

Denise: Eh, Dave's got to come with me to ante-natal classes.

Jim/Antony: Ooooooh.

Jim: What are you going there for, soft lad?

Dave: I've got to learn about everything, haven't I?

Jim: Well, what's there to bloody learn? You feed the bugger when it's hungry, change it's nappy when it's crapped itself – that's all there is to it.

Barbara: Oh, and what do you know? You never came near these two when they were little.

Mary: Joe was the same. I always remember when Cheryl was born, he was terrified of holding her – she was such a delicate little thing. She was only six pounds.

Jim: Who was? Cheryl?

Barbara: (POINTEDLY) Yes.

Mary: They don't stay small for long.

Barbara: No. How's your diet going, Cheryl?

Cheryl: Oh, I've lost half a stone.

Barbara: Have you? Ooh Cheryl, oh, that's wonderful. Aah. Well done.

Denise: That's a load, that, Cheryl.

PAUSE.

Cheryl: No! I don't mean half a stone, I mean half a pound.

Barbara: Ooh.

Denise: Ooh well.

Barbara: Well. That's good in't it – ey, eh it's going in the right direction

Denise: Yeah.

JIM AND DAVE EXCHANGE LOOKS.

Mary: Yes. It's marvellous.

Barbara: Oh, your turn next, Cheryl.

Mary: Yes. All she needs to do now, is find a boyfriend, get married and then conceive.

REFLECTIVE PAUSE. JIM AND DAVE EXCHANGE LOOKS.

Joe: She's got not chance.

Mary: Denise pregnant, and do you know Lorraine in her leggings sterilized!

Barbara: Yeah. I've just been telling our Denise.

Denise: Yeah.

Jim: I tell you what, Joe, we'll have a bloody good night in the Feathers the night the baby's born.

Joe: Right.

Dave: Oh aye – big style.

Denise: You're not going.

Dave: Course I'm going.

Denise: Oh, cheers, you all have a great time, I do all the hard work.

Jim: Well, it'll be the first time you've done any bloody hard work and anyway, he's done his little bit, now, haven't you son?

Barbara: Oh, Jim! Don't spoil it.

Mary: Ooh, they have them in and out of hospitals now, Barbara. Not like it was with us – we were in a week!

Barbara: Yeah. I remember when I came home with our Denise, there wasn't a thing done in the house. Jim hadn't even washed a dish while I'd been in.

Jim: I was leaving them to soak.

Mary: Well, we'd better be going – *The Bill*'s on in a bit. We just wanted to say congratulations. Are you staying, Cheryl?

Cheryl: No, no, I'll have my tea then I'll come back later – will you still be here?

Denise: Yeah.

Cheryl: See you later.

Jim: You don't want to be missing your tea, love. You'll be bloody wasting away.

Mary: Really lovely news.

Denise: Ah, thanks Mary. Bye.

GENERAL 'SEE YOU LATER'.

MARY, JOE AND CHERYL LEAVE.

All: Bye.

Jim: Ta-ta, Joe.

Dave: Bye, Joe.

Jim: Bloody 'ell, I thought they were never going. Tell you what though, Joe was made up about the baby, wasn't he?

All: Yeah.

Dave: Yeah, he was, yeah.

Antony: (JOE STYLE) Aye. A little baby.

DAVE AND ANTONY KILL THEMSELVES LAUGHING.

Jim: Got a great personality though, hasn't he. Apparently the *South Bank Show* are gonna do a one-hour special on him. (THEY ALL LAUGH) Well, they are. (PAUSE. RUBS HIS HANDS) Right, where's me newspaper? I'm off to the khazi to try for a little baby of me own.

Barbara: Jim.

Denise: Dad!

Dave: Eh, be careful of them stairs, grandad.

Jim: Bloody 'ell, yeah. Grandad. (SHOT OF JIM HALFWAY UP THE STAIRS) Keanu my arse.

END OF EPISODE ONE.

Episode 2

SUNDAY LUNCHTIME

DENISE AND NANA ARE SITTING ON THE SETTEE, WATCHING *EASTENDERS*. BARBARA IS SLAVING AWAY IN A STEAMY KITCHEN, UP TO HER ELBOWS IN PANS.

Nana: Denise, there was a woman from Droylsden on Richard and Judy – having a makeover.

Denise: Oh.

Nana: Well it's only ten minutes from me. (SHE CALLS OUT) Barbara!

Barbara (OOV): Yes. (COMES IN, FLUSTERED) What, Mam?

Nana: I was just telling Denise, there was a woman on Richard and Judy from Droylsden. She was having a makeover.

Barbara: Well, what about it?

Nana: Well it's only ten minutes from me. (BARBARA GOES BACK INTO THE KITCHEN) Ooh they did her hair lovely – it was sort of, um, a reddish tint you know, like one of them Red Setter dogs and they did all her make-up and it was all free – and they gave her an outfit to take home. It was for her wedding anniversary and they put her in, eh, like a pastel-blue – do you remember that blue scarf I had Denise?

Denise: Oh, yeah.

Nana: Well, it was that sort of a blue. Blue-ish. (SHOUTS) She knew nothing about it Barbara.

Barbara (OOV): What?

WE MOVE TO THE KITCHEN. ON BARBARA, HASSLED. ANTONY COMES IN THE BACK DOOR.

Antony: Oh great – I'm starving.

Barbara: Set the table for me will you, love.

Antony: I've just come in, why can't Denise do it?

Barbara: 'Cause she's pregnant.

Antony: Yeah, yeah, great excuse.

ANTONY GOES INTO LIVING ROOM.

Antony: Hiya, Nana.

Nana: Hiya, love. Have you been playing your football, Antony?

Antony: Yeah. We won.

Nana: Oh, lovely. I was just telling Denise, there was a woman from Droylsden on Richard and Judy on Friday – having a makeover.

Antony: (LAYING THE TABLE) Oh, right.

Nana: She knew nothing about it – her daughter sorted it out for her anniversary.

Barbara: Where are those two? I told them to be back for two o'clock.

Antony: I'll go and get'em.

Denise: Don't let him go, Mam – he only wants a lager out of 'em. If you let him go, they'll be there all afternoon.

Barbara: Ooh yeah. Yeah, yeah you stay where you are, Antony.

Denise: Antony, you had a shower after footie?

Antony: I'll get one later.

Denise: I'm prone to infections now I'm pregnant. Bet you're riddled with germs. Mam, Antony's full of germs.

Barbara: Wash your hands, Antony.

KEY IN THE DOOR. JIM, DAVE AND TWIGGY COME IN. THEY TAKE THEIR COATS OFF AND PUT THEM ON THE SETTEE.

Jim: And I said to him, I don't care if I win twenty bloody spot the balls, I'm still not buying your ale. Ah, hello, love. How big is it now, eh? Bloody 'ell Norma, is it nearly a week since we last saw you?

Twiggy: Hello, Norma. Looking gorgeous as ever.

Nana: Ah, hello, love.

Twiggy: Why you don't just move in here, I'll never know.

Nana: Well, there's Denise's room.

Dave: Hiya, Nana. (KISSES HER)

Nana: Hiya, love.

Denise: Dave!

Dave: Oh. (KISSES DENISE)

Denise: Ooh, you stink of drink. Lovely.

Twiggy: Ey, Denise, Dave's just told me about the baby – great news that.

Denise: Ah, thanks, Twiggy.

Twiggy: And don't worry about gear for it. I can get all that sort of stuff.

Denise: Oh, I don't want dodgy gear for this baby, Twiggy.

Dave: We do.

Twiggy: I'll tell you what, I'll knock off a cot for the baby. That'll be my present for it.

Nana: Aah. Heart of gold, ain't he.

Jim: (CALLS OUT) Barb, put another plate out, love, Twiggy's here.

BARBARA GRIMACES IN THE KITCHEN AND GOES OUT TO LIVING ROOM.

Barbara: Right. Hi, Twiggy.

Twiggy: That all right, Barbara?

Barbara: Oh yes, there's always plenty of food here, love. Go set another place for Twiggy.

Nana: Eh Twiggy – I believe you've got yourself a nice ladyfriend?

Twiggy: Well, I couldn't wait for you for ever.

Nana: Ooh, go on! Hey, I'm going to be a great grandmother you know – if I live long enough. Antony, tell your mam I don't want too much meat.

ANTONY GOES INTO KITCHEN.

Antony: Mam, Nana says she don't want too much meat.

Barbara: Well nobody's having too much meat. I could swing for your father one of these days. Now tell them to sit up, Antony.

Antony: Right. Dinner's ready.

Twiggy: I'm sitting next to you, Norma.

Nana: Oh, give us a hand then.

Twiggy: Aah, come on love. Y'all right.

Denise: Nana, your bag.

Nana: Oh, ta, love. Where do you want me?

Jim: Next door.

Twiggy: I'll go round there. Don't worry about me Barb. I'll eat any old shite.

Denise: You'll all have to come round to mine and Dave's one time for Sunday dinner.

Jim: Oh, nice one.

Denise: Mam can cook there. Be a nice change for her.

Dave: Ah, yeah.

Nana: That's too much for me, Barbara.

Twiggy: It's all right, I'll polish off anything you can't eat.

Nana: Oh, this gravy looks watery, Barbara. I usually put corn-flour in mine. You've never tasted my gravy, have you, Twiggy?

Denise: Oh, ta.

Twiggy: Can't say I've had that pleasure.

Dave: Hey, Bob the Spark was in the pub, Nana.

Nana: Yeah.

Dave: Said your video'll be ready on Friday.

Nana: Ooh, what's to do with it?

Dave: He doesn't know. He's not had a chance to have a look at it yet.

Nana: Ooh, I'm lost without it.

Jim: You never bloody use it. We always have to record everything for ya.

Nana: Well I like watching Dave and Denise's wedding video on it. D'you know Elsie? Lives next door to me? She's seen it five times.

Jim: Well that must be bloody entertaining, watching a crowd of people you don't know.

Nana: Well she feels like she knows you all. It's company you know when you live on your own.

BARBARA SITS DOWN, HOT AND FLUSTERED.

Jim: All right, Barb?

Barbara: Yes.

Jim: You're as red as a bloody beetroot.

Barbara: It's nothing. Just leave it.

Denise: Ey, Twiggy, who's this new ladyfriend what you've got then?

Twiggy: Eh, she's a tasty piece – I think this could be the one.

All: Aah.

Jim: That's what the three lads said who have kids to her.

Twiggy: Nothing wrong with that.

Jim: Nothing said.

Barbara: Hey, Twiggy, you'll have to bring her round one night and introduce her to us.

Twiggy: Yeah, I'd love to, but she works nights in a petrol station.

Barbara: Oh, does she? Oh, that's a dangerous job in't it for a young girl, working nights in a petrol station.

Jim: You haven't seen her, Barb. Lennox Lewis wouldn't tangle with her.

Twiggy: Yeah, she's well capable of handling herself.

Barbara: Aah.

Jim: Bloody 'ell, Barb, how long have these roasties been in?

Barbara: They were done half an hour ago, but you were still in the pub.

Jim: Well Dave was getting his annual round in and I didn't want to miss that.

Twiggy: How you getting on Denise, now you're not drinking?

Denise: Oh, I'm only not drinking at dinnertime. I'm allowed to drink at night.

Jim: It's all right. The baby'll come out with a lager top.

Nana: Who wants my beef? This is too much for me. The last time I had it, it got stuck under my palate.

Jim: Well that's you all over isn't it Norma – getting a couple of days' worth out the bugger.

Barbara: Jim! Can we have just one Sunday dinner in peace?

Jim: Did you play footie, Antony?

Antony: Yeah, we won.

Jim: Did you take Emma with you?

Antony: Yeah.

Nana: Who's Emma?

Denise: His girlfriend.

Dave: Ooh.

Antony: She's not my girlfriend – she's just a mate.

Nana: Have you met her, Barbara?

Barbara: No.

Jim: No, we probably won't meet her till he puts her up the shoot, then they'll come round here lookin' for a few bob off us.

Barbara: Jim.

Nana: Who's this Emma?

Jim: I'm sure you know her Norma, Emma Royd?

Nana: Who is Emma Royd?

Jim: She lives up your back passage.

ANTONY IS KILLING HIMSELF LAUGHING.

Barbara: Jim! We're trying to eat our dinners here.

Nana: Whose back passage?

Barbara: Mam, take no notice. They're being rude.

Jim: Antony, have a bit of respect for your Nana.

PAUSE.

Nana: Oh Twiggy, did you see *This Morning* the other day? There was a woman on it from Droylsden. She was having a makeover. Droylsden's only ten minutes from me you know. Ooh, I'd love a makeover.

Barbara: Ooh, *I'd* love a makeover.

Jim: Bloody 'ell Barb, the programme's only two-and-a-half hours long. (BARBARA GIVES HIM DAGGERS) Makeover my arse. You're my beautiful rose. That's why I married you.

Barbara: Aah.

Jim: It certainly wasn't for your cooking.

Barbara: Dave?

Dave: Umm.

Barbara: How's that baby's room comin' on?

Dave: Ah, smashing thanks, yeah.

Barbara: That moped still in there is it?

Dave: Yeah.

Denise: You better get that shifted soon, Dave.

Dave: I've got six months to shift that.

Denise: Five months and seventeen days.

Barbara: Aah.

Nana: Oh, I hope I live to see it.

Jim: Oh, you bloody will Norma. Don't worry. You will.

Nana: Betty buried her husband on Wednesday. When I go I don't want to be buried, I want to be cremated.

Barbara: Ah, Mam.

Jim: Just like these roasties?

Nana: Oh I was upset, him going like that.

Barbara: Did you go to the funeral, Mam?

Nana: No, I weren't invited. They wanted to keep it to those who knew him. That's what upset me. (PAUSE) I mean you don't have to have met someone to celebrate their death.

Jim: Well you only go to them bloody funerals so you can go to the buffet.

Nana: Oh, I don't mean to speak ill of the dead, but he were a tight bugger that Kenneth by all accounts. Do you know he used to follow her around Kwik Save taking everything out of her basket as quick as she put it in. He never let her have Jaffa Cakes, only Rich Tea. I bet she'll have Jaffa Cakes now.

JIM SHAKES HIS HEAD

Nana: Do you know Theresa in the post office – her whose husband went grey overnight?

Barbara: Oh, yeah.

Nana: Did you know her daughter had applied to be an air hostess?

Barbara: Yeah.

Nana: She's got in – they got the letter back this week.

Barbara: Which airline?

Nana: Eh? Heathrow, I think.

Barbara: Ooh, how lovely! D'you know I would have loved our Denise to be an air hostess.

Denise: Oh, no way, they're only skivvies making tea in the sky.

Barbara: It's not you know. Much more to it than that. You need languages and you need what to do in a crash and all that.

Jim: I know exactly what she'd do in a bloody crash – she'd shit herself, the same as the rest of us.

Barbara: Jim! No shit please, while we're having dinner.

Nana: I've never been on a plane me, Twiggy. I'm eighty-four years old and I've never even sat on one when it was on the ground.

Jim: Well, bloody 'ell Norma, what would you wanna do that for?

Nana: I'm just saying. Or a helicopter. I've been to Ringway a couple of times and watched them landing and taking off. Me and Elsie had a picnic there before she was housebound. She was fascinated by the airport was Elsie next door.

Denise: Ey, when, 'em, me and Dave went on our honeymoon to Tenerife, right, we was on the plane and we thought it was just gonna be the first drink that was free, but it was all free. Yeah, we was bladdered, weren't we?

Dave: Absolutely hammered.

Denise: It was brilliant.

Antony: Nice one!

Barbara: Aah.

Denise: Ey Nana, you wouldn't like the toilets on them planes – they're tiny.

Nana: Do they have toilets on the planes?

Denise: Yeah.

Jim: Of course they have toilets on the bloody planes.

Denise: How do you know, you've never been on a plane?

Jim: I know and you wouldn't get me on one either.

Twiggy: Safest form of transport that, Jim.

Jim: Eh, I know, you don't read about crashes because they keep it all covered up, but you can't tell me the likes of Richard Branson, whose got his own bloody airline, goes everywhere by balloon, he is not bloody soft is he?

Antony: Hey, he's loaded, he is. He's worth over a billion.

Jim: Bloody 'ell that's only about ten quid less than you, isn't it, Nana?

Dave: D'you know how he started off his business that Branson? From a little record shop.

Barbara: Ooh, can't imagine him behind a record shop can you? With his beard.

Jim: What's his beard got to do with it?

Barbara: Ey, imagine what it must be like to be him. All that money.

Jim: Can't get that rich without being as tight as a camel's arse in a sandstorm, can ya? He wouldn't give you the steam off his piss that fella.

Barbara: Jim! 'Shit' and 'piss' – it's Sunday dinner.

Nana: Well I like Richard Branston me. I've always liked him.

Jim: You don't even know who he is.

Nana: I do, I saw that programme about him and his balloons.

Jim: He's not a bloody children's entertainer.

Antony: He's got his own island, him.

Jim: I know, the tight get.

Nana: Well I like him.

Barbara: Right, pass us your plates. Antony, help us with these plates, will ya love? Who wants pudding?

Twiggy: What is it, Barbara?

Barbara: It's tinned fruit, love.

Twiggy: Oh, great.

Jim: Bloody 'ell, you're pushing the boat out, aren't you Barb.

Nana: What sort of tinned fruit is it, Barbara?

Barbara: Fruit cocktail, Mam.

Nana: Will you take the grapefruit out of mine, I can't eat it. I like it, but it doesn't like me.

Twiggy: Is that right, Norma?

Nana: Puts a road right through me.

Jim: Ah, what a lovely thought that is. Antony, when you come out, bring the squirty cream, will you lad.

Twiggy: Ey, I'll tell you what, my new lady, Debbie, she's a great cook.

Denise: Is she?

Twiggy: Ah yeah, she does a lovely Ruby.

Nana: What does she do Twiggy?

Twiggy: Ruby Murray. Curry.

Nana: Oh, you daft thing!

Denise: Mam.

Mam: Yes.

Denise: Don't forget no juice on mine.

Barbara: Right.

Jim: Little Keanu might like the juice.

Nana: Eh, how are your cravings these days Denise? Is it still Toffee Crisps?

Denise: Yeah. Yeah and sometimes an Aero.

Nana: But you liked them before, didn't you?

Denise: Yeah. Yeah. Yes it's funny, in't it?

Jim: Cravings my arse.

Nana: Ooh, how's Mary, is she still having her dizzy spells?

Barbara: Yeah, well she hasn't had one since Wednesday so she's keeping her fingers crossed.

Nana: D'you remember my dizzy spells, Barbara?

Barbara: Yes, Mam, I do.

Nana: I had a whole spate of dizzy spells when I lost Barbara's dad. I had a fall in the Stretford precinct. It was outside Timpson's. It's still talked of to this day.

Jim: Who talks about it?

Nana: Me and Elsie. Timpson's, do you know where that is, Twiggy? It's erm , opposite the Hallmark card shop. There. Ooh, you do feel awful.

Twiggy: Yeah, well you're all right now girl. That's all that matters.

ANTONY SQUIRTS THE CREAM ON HIS FRUIT COCKTAIL.

Jim: Oh, eh, eh. That'll do. Bloody 'ell. Do you want to think of other people, instead of yourself, self, self all the bloody time? They'll take the taste of the bloody fruit away.

Nana: Got any Carnation, Barbara? That squirty stuff lies heavy on my stomach.

Barbara: Antony, go and see if there's any Carnation in the cupboard.

Antony: Ah, bloody . . .

Nana: Oh, if it's too much trouble, don't bother, I'll go.

Barbara: Antony, will you go and look.

HE LEAVES.

Jim: You all right, Barb. Your face looks like a Belisha Beacon.

Barbara: Will you leave it, Jim, I'm just hot, that's all.

Denise: Hey, Mam, d'ya know what it might be – it might be the menopause.

Barbara: Will you drop it, Denise. I've told ya, I'm just hot.

PAUSE.

Nana: We used to call it the change in my time.

PAUSE. ANTONY COMES BACK IN.

Antony: Sorry Nana, there in't any.

Nana: Ah, never mind. Don't worry, I'll have some of this. Ooh, did you see Dale Winton's home in *OK* magazine? Ooh, it was tidy. It was just like a show home.

Jim: Dale Winton my arse.

Dave: He wouldn't say 'no', Jim.

Barbara: I've given up trying to keep a show home with this lot.

Jim: That's not his real home, he has all sorts of people in to do that.

Twiggy: I like Dale Winton, me.

Antony/Dave/Jim: Whoooooooohh! (LIMP WRISTS)

Denise: Do you know who's got a nursery in *Hello* magazine, exactly like what I'd love, you know Jane Seymour when she had them twins.

Barbara: Ooh.

Denise: And do you know what she'd done, right, she's painted all these animals on it, you know, like a zoo and then she's stuck real toy monkeys on top of it. It looks absolutely gorgeous.

Jim: Well we just stuck a mirror on the wall in Antony's room and then he could see his own monkey's arse any time he wanted to.

Barbara: Well I think it sounds lovely what she's done, Denise, are ya going to do the same?

Denise: I don't know yet. I can't have any ideas for our nursery 'cause he won't move that moped out of there.

Dave: Bloody 'ell, here we go again.

Jim: I hope *Hello* don't come round unexpected, they'll think they've gone to Barry Sheen's.

Nana: Dale Winton's wardrobes were lovely. Do you know they were specially made to fit in with his busy lifestyle. He worked very closely with the designer on them.

Jim: I'll bet he bloody did. That's why he got all them wardrobes for free. I could get all sorts of free wardrobes if I got up to all that malarky.

Barbara: Jim! Why can't you just feel happy for somebody's fitted wardrobes?

Twiggy: He's a cracking show host, Winton, y'know.

Barbara: Yeah.

Antony: Any more of that tinned fruit, Mam?

Barbara: I'm not opening another tin just for you.

Twiggy: Oh well, if you are opening one Barbara . . .

Barbara: I haven't got another tin, Twiggy. I only said it for Antony. Right then, who wants a cup of tea.

All: Yeah.

Barbara: Put the kettle on, Antony.

Twiggy: Here y'a Barbara, have a ciggy.

Barbara: Oh, thanks Twiggy. Eh, Antony, don't forget, Nana likes a china cup.

Antony: I know.

Twiggy: Ey, that was gorgeous, Barbara. I'll be round next week.

BARBARA AND TWIGGY LIGHT UP.

Denise: Mam, give us a little drag of that ciggy.

Dave: No.

Denise: I'm only asking for a little drag.

Dave: No.

Denise: Oh, one little drag on a Sunday dinner's not gonna harm it.

Dave: Course it is. Any smokin's bound to harm it.

Denise: Oh, I'll tell you what, right Dave, I'll do everything for this baby. I'll carry it on me own for nine months, no smoking, no drinking . . .

Dave: No drinking?

Denise: Yeah well. Hardly any. Yeah well, what about you? You can't even be arsed to move that moped out of the box-room to make it into a nursery. Will you tell him, Mam?

Barbara: Oh, don't bring me into it. I'm not getting involved.

Denise: It's all right for you, Dave. Your life hasn't even changed since I've been having this baby. You just do everything like what you've always done, a load of boozing down the pub.

Jim: Ah, bloody 'ell love, what's wrong with you? Dave works bloody hard all week, he's entitled to a little drink on a Sunday.

Nana: Well I don't think so.

Jim: Bloody 'ell, listen to who's talking. You love a bloody drink.

Nana: No I do not. I just have a sherry at Christmas . . .

Jim: I know, champagne at weddings and so and so . . . Bloody 'ell, Norma.

Nana: Tell him, Barbara.

Barbara: Jim.

Nana: I knew a couple who split up last week. Just because he spent too much time in the pub.

Denise: See.

Barbara: Well, which couple's this?

Nana On *Kilroy*.

Jim: Bloody 'ell, do you see what I'm up against, Twiggy. Bloody Kilroy Silk, ey, bloody orange gob. How's that tea going, Antony?

Antony: It's coming.

Denise: I'm not dropping it, Dave. You're getting rid of that bike.

Twiggy: What kind of bike is it, Dave? I'll shift it for you.

Dave: I can't part with it, Twiggy, you know. It's not the money.

Twiggy: What is it?

Dave: We'll, I've had it since I was sixteen, you know . . .

Twiggy: No, the bike you clown.

Dave: It's a Yamaha FS1E.

Twiggy: What, an old Fizzy?

Dave: Yeah.

Twiggy: I can shift that for you, no danger.

Denise: Ah, can you Twiggy? That'd be brilliant.

Dave: Ey, it's my bike. Bloody 'ell, what if you go into labour, want rushing to the hospital.

Jim: The bloody baby'll be reading before you put that bike together again.

Denise: Do you know, ever since I've met him that bike's been in bits. It used to be in bits at his mam's house in the dining room. Now it's in bits in our box-room.

Nana: D'you know, Twiggy, I've never been on a motorbike in my whole life.

Jim: Bloody 'ell, Norma, is there any form of transport you *have* been on?

Nana: I've been on a boat on the lake in Pickmere. We were only supposed to have it out half an hour, but we had it a good forty minutes. Ooh, he was frosty when we took it back.

Barbara: Who was frosty?

Nana: Well the bloke in charge of the boats. Apparently he'd called out our number and we'd forgotten what our number was! I can't remember what number it was now.

Jim: Well try and bloody think will you love, 'cause I won't be able to sleep unless I know.

Nana: Well, I'll say it was forty-something, but I can't quite remember.

Jim: Well what's a bloody boat in Pickmere go to do with Dave's bike? D'ya see what I mean, Twiggy? Come again next week for your dinner lad, the conversation's always as riveting. Bloody 'ell.

Twiggy: I'll tell you what, I'll pop round tomorrow, Dave, and give you a price for that.

Dave: I don't know about that, Twigg.

Denise: I do. We're getting rid of that bike. Oh no, I'm putting my foot down. It's bad Feng Shui to have a bike in bits in your box-room.

Jim: Feng Shui my arse.

Barbara: Good for you, Denise.

Antony: You know what, I reckon you should keep that bike, Dave. Yeah, I do yeah.

Denise: It's nothing to do with you, Antony. Shut your big fat gob, you big fat pig. Mam, will you tell him?

Barbara: Haven't we heard enough about this stupid bike.

DENISE AND DAVE LOOK DAGGERS AT EACH OTHER.

PAUSE.

Nana: I *have* been on a train once or twice, but do you know, Twiggy, my favourite mode of transportation . . .

Jim: Is a bloody broomstick.

Barbara: Jim!

Nana: Ignore him, Barbara. A coach. I like it all, me: the camaraderie, the singing, the whip-round for the driver, the toilet stops . . . People don't get coaches nowadays.

Jim: No. They're frightened in case you get on the bloody thing.

Nana: Oh, shut up.

Antony: Here y'a, Nana.

Nana: Oh, ta love.

Twiggy: Oh, ta lad.

Nana: Barbara, I'll be going home straight after this meal.

Barbara: You not staying for the afternoon, Mam?

Nana: Well I'm hoping I'll need the toilet in about half an hour and I'd rather go home to my own toilet. Nowhere like your own toilet, is there, Twiggy?

Barbara: Do you know, that's all we've had this mealtime. Toilet talk.

Jim: Yeah, but we're only going through the motions.

Nana: Oh, David, I'll need you to take me home. I've got a couple of little jobs I'd like you to look at. (THEY ALL LAUGH) I don't mean that. I wouldn't show David, it's bad enough showing Elsie.

Barbara: What, Elsie next door?

Nana: Well, her sister's a nurse.

PAUSE.

Dave: So what is it you want me to do, Nana?

Nana: Well I'd like you to look at me iron, David, and I've got a tap dripping in the bathroom.

Dave: Oh sound, I'll sort that out.

Denise: Cheers, Dave, yeah. Sort everyone else's houses out.

PAUSE.

Nana: Ooh Barbara, did I tell ya, Elsie's having a shower fitted. She can't get out the bath now for love nor money. Her son-in-law's paying for it and he paid for all the tiling that she had done as well.

Jim: Soft bugger.

Nana: He's very good to her is her son-in-law. Treats her with a lot of respect.

Twiggy: Right, I'll be getting off. Cracking dinner that, Barbara.

Barbara: You're very welcome Twiggy. Any time.

Twiggy: Pleasure to see you, Norma, as ever. I'll pop round tomorrow, Dave, and have a look at your Fizzy.

Dave: Aye, all right pal. I'll sort out the baby's room.

Barbara: Aah, Dave.

Denise: See ya, Twiggy.

Twiggy: Ey, don't you go overdoing it, girl.

Jim: Oh, there's no danger of that is there.

All: See ya, Twiggy.

TWIGGY GOES.

Antony: See ya, Twigg.

Dave: See ya, Twigg.

Jim: Ta-da, pal. One greedy scrounging get that fella, in't he. What a bloody brass neck, fancy coming back here for his Sunday dinner.

Dave: You asked him, Jim.

Jim: I know, but I didn't think he'd say yes.

Barbara: Do you know, Jim! You've got more faces than the town hall clock.

Nana: And every one of em's miserable.

EVERYONE CHEERS.

Jim: I tell you what, I'll give you that one, Norma.

Nana: And every one of em's miserable!

Jim: All right, don't bloody milk it.

Nana: Oh, you know what, I reckon that hot tea's beginning to work me. I won't want you to take me home, David. I'll go and have a try now and, eh, if it's all right, I'll be able to stay this afternoon Barbara.

Jim: Ah, fantastic news.

Barbara: Shall I get you a paper, Mam?

Nana: Oh, yes please, love. I'd like to take the *People* and, 'em, and the *News of the World* and, 'em, have you got that free newspaper, I like looking at that. Ah, ta love.

Jim: Bloody 'ell Norma, how constipated are you, girl? You've got half of bloody Fleet Street under your arm, haven't ya. Eh, if the world's press could see you now. Anyway, give us a shout when you're finished.

Nana: Why, do you want it after me, Jim?

Jim: No, I want to phone Dyno-Rod.

JIM FLICKS THE REMOTE.

END OF EPISODE TWO.

Episode 3

BARBARA AND JIM WATCH TV.

Barbara: Ooh. Ainsley Harriott's bathroom. Oh Jim, put BBC on – it's *Changing Rooms*.

Jim: I'm watching that.

Barbara: You're not, you're reading the paper.

Jim: Yes, I'm *reading* the paper, but I'm *listening* to that.

Barbara: No, put *Changing Rooms* on.

Jim: (TUTS) Bloody 'ell, what did your last slave die of? (HE PRESSES THE REMOTE) Bloody 'ell, if you call that entertainment, watching a Cockney knocking nails into plywood, I don't know, is that what it's come to?

Barbara: Shut up, Jim.

Jim: Hard to believe it. Look at him, the bloody old nancy-boy tie-dyeing the neighbour's bloody curtains . . . I'm glad we don't pay our licence fee, that's all I can say.

Barbara: We do. I pay it.

Jim: You what?

Barbara: Jim, they've got detector vans now.

Jim: Detector vans, my arse.

Barbara: Ooh, they come and park outside your house, they even know which programme you're watching.

Jim: Yes well, they wouldn't charge us if they knew we were watching that shite. Bloody *Changing* bloody *Rooms*. More like changing bloody channels.

Barbara: Well I like seeing people's houses get done up. It's very popular is this, Jim.

Jim: Why don't they do an hour and a half's film of me emulsioning the bloody box-room?

Barbara: Huh! When was the last time you did any decorating?

Jim: Well I'm waiting for them *Changing Room* clowns, aren't I? Eh? Like them two there, they're doing bugger all, just sitting on their arses.

Barbara: I'd be ashamed to let anybody come to this house.

PAUSE. THEY WATCH – WE SEE LAWRENCE.

Jim: I wouldn't let old nancy-boy round here for a kick-off.

Barbara: Ooh. I think I might stencil our kitchen unit.

Jim: Stencil my arse. (POINTS) He would, there's nothing he'd like better than to stencil my arse.

Barbara: I wish he would. That'd keep you quiet.

Jim: Um. Nothing he'd like better.

Barbara: D'you know, Jim, you've no imagination, this house could be lovely.

Jim: Why what's wrong with it? It's like a bloody show-home, isn't it?

Barbara: Um!

DOOR GOES.

Jim: Quick! Hide the telly, Barb, it might be a detector van.

BARBARA GOES TO THE DOOR.

Jim: Smillie my arse.

Denise: Hiya.

Barbara: Hiya, you all right.

Denise: Yeah, you all right.

Barbara: Yeah.

Denise: Aah.

Barbara: Hiya.

Dave: Y'all right, Barbara.

Barbara: Y'all right, Dave.

Jim: Bloody 'ell, that's the last thing we want. Torvill and Dean back again. Eh?

DENISE AND DAVE COME IN, SAY 'HIYA' AND SIT DOWN.

Denise: Hiya, Dad.

Jim: Sit down kids!

Dave: Hiya, Jim.

Jim: I haven't seen you two since, em? When was the last time I saw you two? Must have been last night, wasn't it? Bloody 'ell. Anyway, don't sit still for too long or your mother will bloody stencil ya!

Denise: Oh, is it *Changing Rooms*?

Barbara: Yeah.

Denise: Oh, I love this.

Barbara: Yeah, so do I.

PAUSE.

Barbara: Ooh, Denise. Ooh, I like those. Oh. Aren't they lovely.

Denise: Do you?

Barbara: Yeah. Catalogue?

Denise: Market, £7.99.

Barbara: Oh ey, Jim, market, £7.99. Oh you are with it our Denise. Oh God, Denise, I nearly forgot, you've been for your ante-natal?

Denise: Oh yeah.

Barbara: How did you get on?

Denise: Well, it was all a bit weird really. This midwife woman what was running it, she said that we had to talk a bit about our partners, and our partners had to talk a bit about us.

JIM'S FACE.

Barbara: What did Dave say about you?

Denise: Well he just said that I was pregnant.

Jim: Bloody 'ell. That must have been a shock for the rest of the ante-natal class, wasn't it? Bloody 'ell.

THEY ALL LAUGH.

Denise: I didn't really know what to say about Dave. I just said about you know his disco and about the removals that he does 'n' that. But there isn't much else to say about him really.

Barbara: No.

Dave: No.

Denise: Oh yeah, and I said about how long we'd been together.

Dave: How long is it now?

Denise: Five years.

Dave: Five years, yeah.

Jim: Bloody 'ell, they must have been clinging on to every word were they?

Barbara: You're a sarcastic sod, you are, Jim.

Jim: I'm not. I bet you people were just glad they were out there able to see them instead of being stuck in here watching bloody paint dry like that.

Denise: What's up with you, crabby arse?

Barbara: Take no notice of him, Denise. He's been like this all day.

Denise: Why?

Barbara: 'Cause I told him Nana's coming to stay for a week.

Jim: It's not definite yet.

Barbara: Oh yes it is.

Denise: Dad! She's having a cataract removed.

Jim: A cataract. What's she having it removed for? If she hasn't seen everything now, by the time she's bloody eighty-bloody-four, what else is there left for her to look at.

Barbara: Jim. It's a very serious operation. She's only coming for a week.

Jim: A bloody week! Once she gets her big fat flabby arse on that settee, she'll be there for the duration.

Dave: It'll be company for you Jim, while Barbara's at work. You know Norma's never stuck for summit to say.

Jim: Well if you've done the little box-room, why don't you take her to stay with you?

Denise: I'd love to have Nana staying with us.

Dave: No way.

Barbara: D'you lot . . . ? This is my mother we're talking about here. You can't leave her on her own, when she's not well with no one to talk to.

Jim: It's a shame the cataract's not on her tongue.

Barbara: All right. That'll do Jim.

Jim: Is there any chance of a brew here?

Barbara: Well our Antony isn't here. He's gone out with Emma.

Jim: Well what time will he be back? I'm bloody gagging here.

Barbara: I don't know. He won't be late. Ey, our Denise, you should see her. She's only seventeen you know and she's got a car. Tiny little thing she is.

Denise: She's got her own car?

Barbara: Yeah.

Denise: What's she doing with our Antony then?

Barbara: Oh, I don't know.

Dave: Antony going out with a bird with a car, eh?

Jim: She's the one that needs the cataract operation, eh? Who'd want to go out with our Lurch?

Denise: What's she look like?

Barbara: She looks like one of the Spice Girls, you know.

Denise: Does she?

Barbara: Um. Oh ey, Denise, she's got her nose pierced.

Jim: Bloody 'ell. Piggy Spice.

Denise: Dave.

Dave: Umm.

Denise: Why don't you take your coat off?

Dave: I'm all right.

Denise: You may as well take it off, Dave.

Dave: It's all right. I'm okay.

Denise: Why don't you just take it off?

Dave: I'm fine with it on.

Barbara: Take your jacket off, Dave.

Dave: No, I'm okay, Barbara.

Barbara: You won't feel the benefit you know when you go out.

Dave: It doesn't matter.

Denise: Why don't you just take it off?

Jim: Take your bloody jacket off will you, Dave.

Dave: Bloody 'ell.

Jim: Bloody 'ell's right.

Dave: I was all right there with that on.

Barbara: Much better.

Denise: See.

BIG PAUSE. THEY WATCH TELLY.

Denise: Dave.

Dave: Um.

Denise: We could strip the floorboards in our kitchen.

Dave: You're joking aren't you? It's good lino we've got in there.

Jim: You don't want to be doing that, love. You don't want to be getting splinters in your bloody feet while you're dashing over a hot stove. Has she, eh, she cooked you a little meal yet, Dave?

Dave: Not a meal.

Denise: Dad. Dave has his dinner at the chippy. He doesn't need a big meal when he comes in.

Jim: Ah, just as well, eh.

Denise: Ooh, look at masterchef. You've never ever cooked a meal either.

Dave: Eh, you're all right though, he'll get plenty of practice next week making dinners for him and Norma.

Jim: Aye, you're bloody right there. The only time she's quiet is when she's got her gob full.

A CAR PULLS UP OUTSIDE.

Denise: Oh, bet that's our Antony.

Dave: Oh, let's have a look. Oh, it is him. It is him.

DAVE AND DENISE ARE AT THE WINDOW.

Denise: Ah. Ah, he's kissing her.

Dave: Hey, she looks all right her.

Denise: Yeah.

Dave: Nice set of alloys.

Denise: I like her hair. Why is *she* going out with our Antony? Oh he's getting out! He's getting out, he's getting out.

Dave: He's getting out.

Barbara: He's getting out, Jim.

Denise: Oh no, he's still talking to her – oh, look at him, with his hand on the roof, leaning in the window. He's coming.

DENISE AND DAVE QUICKLY SIT DOWN. PAUSE. ANTONY COMES IN. THEY ALL SING 'THAT'S AMORE'.

Dave: Eh, nice little car that, Ant. Is it comfy on the back seat?

Antony: How old are you lot?

Jim: Okay, Romeo, now get the kettle on. We're all bloody parched here.

Denise: Why didn't you bring her in, Antony?

Antony: Well why d'you think?

Barbara: Antony, you're back early aren't you, love?

Antony: Well, yeah, Emma's got an exam tomorrow.

Denise/Dave/Jim: Whooooooh.

Dave: Eleven plus?

Jim: Ey, where's she from, Lurch?

Antony: Altrincham.

Jim: Ooh. Hey Barb, we'll be made up when they're married, won't we.

Antony: You're worse than a bunch of kids you lot.

Jim: (TO ANTONY) I thought you were gonna put the kettle on.

Antony: All right, who wants a brew?

Jim: Every-bloody-body. God, see what happens when you fall in love, it makes you dead lazy.

ANTONY GOES INTO KITCHEN.

THEY WATCH TELLY. PAUSE.

Barbara: Have you had your teas?

Denise/Dave: Yes.

Barbara: What did you have?

Denise: Spaghetti.

Barbara: Bolognese?

Denise: Hoops.

Barbara: Oh. We had chops.

Denise: Did you?

Barbara: Yeah.

Jim: Bloody big thick ones like that. (PAUSE) How's work going, Dave?

Dave: It's no good – the money's hopeless.

Jim: They're only paying you from the neck down, see.

Dave: I had a nightmare today moving this woman who was just splitting up from her husband. We were shifting the stuff out into the van, he was coming out taking it all back in again. I hate handling divorces.

Jim: Bloody 'ell, Dave, you're not Petro-bloody-celli son, you're just a furniture remover.

Dave: I know, but she was crying and all sorts.

Barbara: Aah, was she?

Dave: Yeah. We had to hang around ages waiting for a brew, you know, till she stopped crying.

Denise: Aaah.

Barbara: Aah, in't it awful?

Denise: What were they splitting up over?

Dave: I didn't really go that deep into it.

Barbara: Ooh, it's terrible really, in't it?

Denise: Yeah.

Dave: Umm.

Barbara: They're splitting up and there's our Antony finding love.

ANTONY COMES OUT WITH THE TEA.

All: Ah.

Jim: Thank you, Lurchio.

Barbara: Thanks, love.

Antony: Ey, Denise, eh, are you goin' down there tomorrow?

Denise: Where?

Antony: Kissing me arse.

Barbara: Eh, I hope you don't say things like that to Emma.

Jim: Tell you what she's a lucky girl that Emma. She's landed on her feet with you all right, hasn't she, eh? What with your prospects, is it gonna be Burger King, McDonald's, who knows? I bet they must have riveting bloody conversations. I hope she likes *The Simpsons*.

Barbara: Do you know who your dad reminds me of in *The Simpsons*?

EVERYONE LAUGHS. 'WAAAY'. JIM GIVES BARBARA A DIRTY LOOK.

Denise: Who?

Barbara: Homo.

Dave: Homo.

Barbara: Ooh, look at his face. He doesn't like it when we laugh at him, does he?

Jim: They're laughing at you, you dopy bugger. It's not Homo, it's Homer.

Barbara: Hey, any biscuits, Ant?

Antony: No, there was none in the barrel.

Barbara: Go and have a look in the secret cupboard.

Denise: (POINTING AT TEA) Dave.

DAVE PASSES DENISE HER TEA.

Dave: Careful.

Denise: Ta.

ANTONY GOES TO KITCHEN AND SHOUTS THROUGH.

Antony (OOV): Shall I open the Wagon Wheels?

Jim/Dave/Barbara: No.

Denise: Yeah.

Antony: Kit-Kats?

Denise/Jim/Barbara/Dave: No.

Jim: Bring us a Penguin.

Denise: Can't we open them all?

Barbara: I'm only opening one packet. If I open more than one packet it'll get ate. That's the trouble in this house – every time I open something it disappears.

Denise: The baby wants a Wagon Wheel.

Barbara: Aah. (SHOUTS TO ANTONY) Antony, open the Wagon Wheels, don't open the Kit-Kats. Some Penguins and some Club biscuits already open.

Dave: (SHOUTS TO ANTONY) Ey, and save some biscuits for next week for Nana and Homo.

Barbara What did I call Homo before?

Dave: Homer.

Barbara: Oh yeah, oh what am I like? (TO ANTONY) Eh just one.

ANTONY COMES IN WITH BISCUITS.

Barbara: Do you want one, Dave?

Dave: Oh yeah, I'll have a Club, please, ta.

Barbara: (TO DENISE) Wagon Wheel. (TO JIM) Penguin.

Jim: Thank you.

Barbara: I'll have this one.

Dave: (SINGS) 'If you like a lot of chocolate on your biscuit join our Club.'

DENISE LAUGHS.

Jim: 'If you're feeling p-p-p-peckish, p-p-p-pick up a Penguin!'

Barbara: (SINGS) 'Only the crumbliest, flakiest chocolate, tastes like chocolate never tasted before.'

Jim: Who remembers this one? (SINGS) 'She flies like a bird in the sky . . .'

Jim/Dave/Denise/Barbara: (ALL JOIN IN) 'She flies like a bird and I wish that she was mine. She flies like a bird, oh me, oh my I've seen her fly, now I know, I can't let Maggie go.'

Jim: For two points Dave, what was that advert for?

Dave: Nimble. 'Real bread, but lighter.'

Jim: Correct.

Dave: Whooh.

Jim: Correct, young man.

PAUSE. THEY ALL EAT CHOCOLATE BISCUITS.

Jim: Do you know what the best advert was, bar none: Cadbury's Smash. (ROBOT'S VOICE) 'We peel them with our steely knives.'

Barbara: Aah, you know the one I like best, that tea ad with all the chimps.

All: Ah yeah.

Barbara: How do they get them to do that, Jim?

Jim: I don't know, but I tell you what, I wish I could get them chimp trainers to spend a couple of weeks with our Antony teaching him to make a proper bloody brew.

PAUSE.

Denise: Dave.

Dave: Umm.

Denise: Finished now.

DAVE PUTS DENISE'S CUP ON THE TABLE.

Denise: I'm dying for a wee.

Barbara: Bet you're going loads now aren't you, now you're pregnant.

Denise: Yeah. It's knackering me out.

Barbara: Why don't you go now and get it over with?

Denise: I've just got comfy.

Barbara: Aah. You know I'd go for you if I could, don't ya?

Denise: Yeah, thanks.

PAUSE.

Barbara: What've you been doing today?

Denise: I've been dead busy.

Barbara: Ooh, so have I. (PAUSE). Ey, did you see *Jerry Springer*?

Denise: Yeah, I was dead mad, 'cause I fell asleep and missed *Pet Rescue*.

Barbara: Oh.

Jim: Bloody 'ell, it'll be like that here next week when your nana's here. It'll be bloody *Trisha*, then *Kilroy*, then Richard and Judy.

Barbara: Ooh, and don't forget Jim, you'll have to tape *Kilroy* for her if she's watching *Trisha* – or the other way round.

Jim: Bloody 'ell, is she gonna watch all these with just the one eye?

Barbara: Well she can't have both her cataracts done at the same time, can she?

Jim: So she's gonna be staying here again when she has the other one done?

Barbara: Yes.

Jim: Bloody hell fire.

Antony: Dave, how d'you go about getting a gig in the Feathers?

Barbara: Antony, you haven't told them about your new venture.

Dave: What is it?

Antony: Well, I'm managing a band.

DENISE, DAVE AND JIM LAUGH.

Jim: Bloody 'ell. It's Brian Epstein.

Dave: A band.

Denise: You're managing a band? Who's in it?

Antony: Well Darren's on bass, Ryan's singing and Tiggsy's on drums.

Denise: Little Tiggsy on drums!

Antony: Yeah. Well, more of a drum machine. But yeah.

Dave: I've gotta see this.

Antony: Can you get us a gig at the Feathers or what?

Dave: Well you're the manager, aren't you? Anyway what do they sound like?

Antony: Sort of a cross between Oasis and the Manics.

Dave: What sort of stuff do they do?

Antony: Ah well, we do a cover of Wonderwall and eh, a song Ryan wrote about his son – 'Access All Areas'.

Barbara: Ryan's never seen his son.

Antony: Well yeah, that's what the song's about – he can't get access.

Barbara: Aah.

Dave: Bloody 'ell.

Denise: So what's the name of this band then?

Antony: Oh yeah, Exit.

EVERYBODY LAUGHS.

Antony: No. All right, listen, no listen right. It's a marketing thing, yeah, right. Wherever we play our name's up in lights.

Barbara: Hey Antony, that's really clever.

Jim: Exit my arse.

Dave: So, is there only three in this band then?

Antony: No, there's Ryan's brother 'n'all.

Dave: What does he play?

Antony: Well nowt, he's just gonna be dancing on stage, y'know, like Bez out of the Happy Mondays – for a gimmick thing.

Dave: What're you having that for? You don't want Lewis at the side of the stage just arsing about, do you?

Antony: No, not really, but we have to – they're his amps what we use.

Dave: Ooh, bloody 'ell. Ey, I've got a gig for you. You can play at our christening.

Antony: Nice one.

Denise: Get lost, Dave. I'm not having Exit playing 'Access All Areas' at our baby's christening.

Dave: Oh well, I'd have give you the gig, Ant.

Denise: Dave! I've told you, I'm having my Charlotte Church tape at the christening – not that bunch of no-marks.

Barbara: Well I think they sound great.

Denise: Have you heard 'em, Mam?

Barbara: No, but I like anything musical.

Denise: Our Antony, you're only being the manager 'cause you can't play anything. What else does this job entail, Antony?

Antony: Well, you know, just looking after them really. Making sure they get gigs, sorting out contracts with record companies 'n'that, you know.

Jim: You'll be down the front won't you, holding all the groupies back you know, when Ryan's brother's givin' it all that . . .

Denise: Isn't Tiggsy still doing his community service?

Antony: Yeah. But he's only got another year to go.

Jim: Well you'll have to sort it all out. You can't be conquering America and him having to come back home every bloody weekend to do his community service.

Dave: Have you got any tapes?

Antony: Yeah, we're gonna do a demo as soon as Tiggsy's mam will let us use the garage.

Jim: Well you're right there. No use wasting money on bloody Abbey Road if Joan will lend you the garage.

Denise: Well you don't want to be having Ryan singing – he hasn't got anything about him, him.

Barbara: Ah, Ryan. A father at fifteen.

Antony: Thing is, we really need to be, eh, having a gig you know, to get the A&R men to come down. Can't you ask at the Feathers can you, Dave?

Jim: Oh they're gonna bloody love that, aren't they, all the bloody Cockney wideboys sitting there with their ponytails and daft old Ernie standing by the bar screaming for his own tankard.

Barbara: In't it funny how he'll only drink out of his own tankard?

Jim: Well, he's only like your mother with that china cup.

Barbara: Oh, I knew we'd have to get back to *my* mother.

Jim: Okay Dave, shall we nip down the Feathers and get a gig for Boyzone there.

Antony: No. We've not practised enough yet.

Jim: Well shove it up your arse then. You try to bloody help and look at that.

Denise: I'm still dying for a wee.

Barbara: Well go then.

Denise: Well, I may as well wait till we get home.

Dave: (TO JIM) Shall we go down the Feathers then Jim, yeah?

Denise: Dave, you're going nowhere.

Jim: Hey Denise, you know them new trousers, they look bloody awful.

Denise: Look at you in that manky vest, you're hardly Bruce Willis in *Die Hard*.

PAUSE.

Denise: I'm dying for a wee.

Jim: Will you *go* for a piss!

END OF EPISODE THREE.

Episode 4

'That's just there for effect, innit'

Time for a ciggy

Joe   Mary

Dad

Dave and Denise

Nana

Antony

'Look at you in that manky vest, you're hardly Bruce Willis in *Die Hard*'

'Jim! We're trying to eat our dinners here'

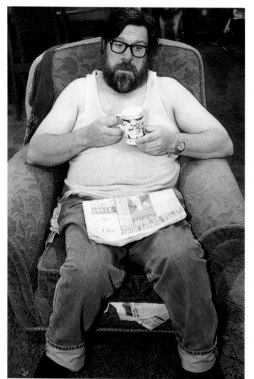

'We're pregnant'

'Denise, there was a woman from Droylsden
on Richard and Judy – having a makeover'

Eating for two

Antony gets a girlfriend   Caught in the middle

'I'd just like to say thanks to everyone for coming. Er. . . thanks'

'To Antony James Royle – my son and heir to the whole of this estate'

Christmas in front of the telly

NANA IS ASLEEP ON THE SOFA, A PATCH OVER ONE EYE. DAVE SITS NEXT TO HER, WATCHING THE TELLY. JIM IS IN HIS CHAIR. JIM QUIETLY TRUMPS AND WAFTS IT TOWARDS NANA. DAVE CLOCKS THIS AND LAUGHS.

CUT TO KITCHEN:

BARBARA IS WASHING UP UNAIDED, AS DENISE SITS AT THE TABLE DRINKING TEA AND FLICKING THROUGH THE CATALOGUE.

Denise: It's not worth buying maternity ones – I mean, I'm not gonna have another – no way.

Barbara: How are you and Dave getting on?

Denise: Well, I don't think he realizes what work it is for me carrying another person around. Ah, Mum, I was looking in that baby book – guess what size it is now.

Barbara: What size?

Denise: The size of an orange.

Barbara: An orange. Oooh, Denise, how lovely.

PAUSE.

Denise: Aaah, Mam, I feel dead sad when I see Nana with that patch on her eye.

Barbara: She was looking in there for baby things for you.

Denise: Aaah, was she? With just one eye?

Barbara: Yeah. She said they were all too dear, though – the thought was there.

Denise: D'you think she'll stay more than the week, Mam?

Barbara: Well, she wants to. I daren't say anything to your dad yet. He'll hit the roof. Oh, you know, you should have seen your dad before – your nana went upstairs with the remote control by mistake, in her handbag.

Denise: Ooh, no. Poor Nana.

Barbara: And, last night she made him take out take all the plugs y'know. She said she couldn't sleep with them all in. He had to reset the video this morning and the air was blue. I wished it was her ears that were covered up.

Denise: Yeah, it's a shame I'm pregnant, I could've come and took her out one afternoon.

Barbara: Aah, you still needing your naps in the afternoon?

Denise: Yeah.

CUT TO LIVING ROOM.

Jim: Oh aye, you know where the bloody thing ended up, don't you? Bloody Cyclops had it in her handbag, didn't she. We had the couch turned over and everything. She's like a bloody vulture.

PAUSE. THEY WATCH TELLY.

Jim: She's had the same bloody handkerchief up her sleeve for four days. (PAUSE) I'd love to have a look in that handbag. We may as well have a mongrel because all she does is eat, shit and sleep. (PAUSE) You see that eye-patch? That could come off now. That's just there for effect, innit. Never mind, (RUBS HIS HANDS IN GLEE) only a couple more days then she'll be away, off to her own bloody place.

Dave: Eh, then there's the other eye though, in't there, Jim?

Jim: Eh, don't be saying that, will you lad.

PAUSE.

Jim: (CONSPIRATORIAL) Dave, d'you fancy a beer tonight?

Dave: Oh, yeah.

Jim: Well look, I'm already in Barbara's bad books, so when she comes in, you mither me. OK?

Dave: But Denise'll go mad at me then though, Jim.

Jim: Oh, don't worry about her. I'll sort her out. That's no problem.

NANA GIVES A GENTLE LITTLE SNORE.

Jim: No sweeter sound, is there? I'd love to strangle the old cow.

CUT TO KITCHEN. ANTONY COMES IN FROM THE HALLWAY.

Antony: Can I have a butty or something, Mam, I'm starving?

Barbara: You've just had chops and chips!

Antony: That was ages ago.

Barbara: Oh, get yourself a Club biscuit. Just one.

Antony: (OF DENISE) *She* comes round here eating and *she's* got her own house. She's always scoffing.

Denise: I'm eating for two. Mam, will you tell him?

Barbara: Yeah, Antony, shut it. Don't you think I've got enough to think about with your dad and your nana without you two starting.

CHERYL COMES IN THROUGH THE BACK DOOR.

Cheryl: Hiya.

Denise: Hiya, Cheryl.

Cheryl: Hiya, Antony.

Denise: Y'all right, Cheryl?

Cheryl: Yeah. How are you?

Denise: Aah, you know, just trying not to overdo it really.

Barbara: Denise, have you told Cheryl?

Denise: About what?

Barbara: What size it is now.

Denise: Oh, yeah. Cheryl, guess what size it is now?

Cheryl: Dunno.

Denise: The size of an orange.

Cheryl: An orange! And I'm godmother to that orange.

Denise: Ooh, yeah.

Barbara: Eh, Cheryl. How are you getting on at Weight Watchers?

Cheryl: Brilliant thanks. I'm doing really well.

Barbara: Ooh. D'you want a biscuit?

Cheryl: Yeah. I can cut something out tomorrow. That's how we do it at Weight Watchers.

Denise: Is it?

Cheryl: You can have stuff – and then cut things out, y'know, the next day or something.

Barbara: Ooh, that's very good in't it? Ey, your mum was telling me she's had to buy you a blender.

Denise: You got a blender, Cheryl?

Cheryl: Yeah.

Denise: Mam. I must get a blender.

Barbara: Ooh, yes.

Denise: What d'you do with it?

Cheryl: It's like you blend up a load of vegetables and it's only eighteen calories a cup. But it tastes horrible.

Denise: That's good though, in't it – eighteen calories.

Cheryl: Yeah. (BITES THE CLUB) There's a hundred and fifty in these.

Barbara: In a Club! Oooh.

Denise: In a Club? Well, if there's eighteen calories in a cup of vegetables, you know, when you weigh up, you could have loads really – just to equal one Club, couldn't you.

Cheryl: Yeah – but I love the chocolate on Club.

Barbara: Oooh.

Denise: Yeah.

BIG PAUSE.

Cheryl: How's your nana's eye?

Denise: We don't know, she won't take the patch off.

Barbara: They said she could, but I think she's leaving it on to annoy Jim.

Denise: (OF THE CATALOGUE) Aah. Look at that.

Cheryl: Aaah, look at that lovely little baby.

GENERAL AAAHS.

Denise: Ey, Cheryl, guess what we're getting. One of them baby intercoms, so if we're downstairs we don't have to go all the way up – y'know, to tell it to shut up and that.

Barbara: God, I didn't need an intercom with you two. I could hear you all over the house.

Cheryl: Antony, are you still seeing Emma?

Antony: Why? Are you after me now?

Cheryl: As if.

Barbara: Antony! Yes, Cheryl, he is still seeing Emma. It's a wonder anybody's going out with you, Antony Royle. Why can't you answer a civil question?

Cheryl: When are you bringing her round?

Antony: I'm not bring her here.

Barbara: We're not the Addams Family, Antony.

PAUSE.

Cheryl: Did your nana find her watch?

Denise: Yeah.

Cheryl: Where was it?

Denise: In her handbag.

Barbara: Ooh, do you know, Denise, let me tell you something. I'd done your nana's washing and I went to hang it on the line, but she wouldn't let me hang her knickers out. She didn't want your dad to see them. I had to cover them up with a tea towel.

THEY ALL LAUGH.

Antony: You should've used a sheet, the size of Nana's knickers.

ANTONY GOES INTO THE LIVING ROOM.

Cheryl: Has Antony dyed his hair?

Denise/Barbara: Yeah.

Cheryl: I thought he had.

CUT TO LIVING ROOM:

Dave: All right, Ant. How's the band?

Antony: They've split up.

Dave: Bloody 'ell.

Jim: (LAUGHS) Exit Exit.

GOOD LONG PAUSE. CAMERA STAYS ON THEM AS THEY WATCH THE TELLY.

CUT TO KITCHEN:

Denise: Ey, right, did anyone see that film last night about the tattoos?

Barbara: No.

Denise: It was absolutely brilliant. There was this bloke, right, and he was obsessed with this woman what was a model and he kidnapped her and he drugged her and then he covered her whole body from the neck downwards with a tattoo.

Barbara: Did she not like it?

Denise: No.

Barbara: I'd hate that to happen to me.

Cheryl: What happened at the end?

Denise: When he'd completely finished her tattoo, right, he took his clothes off and he had a matching body tattoo – and then they were doing it, and his tattoo and her tattoo mingled into one.

Cheryl: Did they?

Denise: But then she grabbed the tattoo gun and stabbed him with it.

Barbara: Oooh.

Cheryl: Blimey.

Denise: There was all ink everywhere.

Barbara: Ooh, what a thing to happen.

Cheryl: I'd love another Club if you've got one, Barbara.

CUT TO LIVING ROOM:

Dave: He tattooed the whole of her body.

Jim: What, boobs 'n'all?

Dave: Oh, the full monty.

Jim: Well, I don't see the point of that? You'd wanna be looking at them, not covering them up.

Dave: My point exactly, James.

BARBARA COMES IN AND SITS DOWN.

Barbara: Aaah, she still asleep?

Jim: Yeah. She's got jaw-ache, God love her.

Barbara: Y'all right, Dave?

Dave: Yeah.

Barbara: You had your tea?

Dave: No, I'm gonna stop for some chips on't way home. Denise couldn't be bothered cooking me owt.

Barbara: Well don't forget, she *is* pregnant.

Jim: Bloody 'ell, Barbara, there's no chance of us forgetting is there? (LOOKS AT NANA) I don't know where she inherits this lazy streak from.

PAUSE.

Barbara: Ooh, ey, Dave, Denise has just been telling us about that film last night.

Dave: Did you watch it, Barbara?

Barbara: No.

Dave: Brilliant it was. This bloke kidnapped this woman and drugged her, then tattooed her from the neck down.

Barbara: Ooh, in't awful – when you weigh up? Was she a young girl, Dave?

Dave: Oh yeah. She was a model.

Jim: Was she? What was it called?

Dave: *Tattoo.*

Jim: 'Hey, Boss, the plane.'

DAVE LAUGHS.

Barbara: Oh, was he in it? That little dwarfy one?

Dave: No.

CHERYL AND DENISE COME IN.

Cheryl: I'm going now, Barbara. I've just come in to have a look at Nana.

Barbara: She's sleeping.

Jim: Whatever you do, don't wake her up.

PAUSE. CHERYL LOOKS AT NANA.

Cheryl: Aah, is that the eye she's had the cataract taken out of?

Jim: No, it's the other one. She's wearing that patch to help her stop smoking. Course it's that bloody eye.

Barbara: Jim! Ignore him, love.

Jim: Ey, you don't want to take her up the precinct for a couple of weeks, do you?

Cheryl: I'm going back now – I've got to blend some vegetables for my supper.

Barbara: Lovely. See ya, Cheryl.

Cheryl: See ya. See ya, Denise.

Denise: See ya, Cheryl.

Jim: Goodnight, Shegsy, love.

CHERYL LEAVES.

Jim: Very dynamic, that Cheryl. (PAUSE). What's all this about blending vegetables?

Denise: Well she's just joined Weight Watchers.

Jim: Weight Watchers? A room full of fat-arsed women paying loads of money to be told not to shovel food into their gobs.

PAUSE.

Barbara: Seems to be sticking to it, though, doesn't she?

Denise: Yeah.

Barbara: Mary was saying she'd had to get in all these low-fat spreads and all sorts. She's got her own compartment in the fridge.

Jim: What's it called – the freezer?

Barbara: Look at your nana. She's worn out, you know. Don't they get more like children when they get older . . . Funny when you think about it, they look after you, then you look after them . . .

Dave: (HAS PICKED UP THE PAPER) There's nowt on the box. (BLOWS OUT) Jim?

Jim: Yes, Dave.

Dave: Do you fancy coming down the Feathers for a pint?

Jim: Yeah, I don't mind, but it's not fair on Barbara.

DAVE LOOKS CONFUSED.

Barbara: Oh, Jim.

Dave: Well, shall we just go for the last hour then?

Jim: Yeah, okay, it's up to Barbara.

Barbara: Ooh, we're having a nice time here aren't we? There's no need for you to go out.

Denise: You don't need to go out, Dave. We're having a nice time here.

Dave: I just thought I'd take your dad out for a drink.

Denise: He doesn't want to go – he's just said.

Barbara: No, he doesn't want to go, Dave.

DAVE LOOKS AT HIM, JIM LOOKS AWAY AT THE TELLY. DAVE LOOKS HURT.

Denise: Antony, what's up with your face?

Antony: Nowt.

Barbara: You not seeing Emma tonight, Antony?

Antony: No.

Dave: Where is she?

Antony: She's gone to the pictures with a friend.

Dave: What, a girl?

Antony: No. A lad. Her family and this other family have been really close. It's just a mate, that's all.

Dave, Denise and Jim all scoff: 'AAAARRRGGGHH'.

Denise: (SINGS) 'Torn between two lovers, (DAVE AND JIM JOIN IN) feeling like a fool, loving both of you is breaking all the rules . . .'

Antony: Shut it. You're doing my head in, you lot.

Barbara: Leave him. You don't know that.

Jim: Ey, I wouldn't have that, Antony lad.

Antony: It's just a mate of hers.

Dave: Oh aye. He'll be in the cinema with her now with a big box of popcorn on his lap with a hole cut in t'bottom, offering her some. Know what I'm saying?

Antony: You mean like you did with Beverly Macca?

Denise: Mam! Why does he always have to bring Beverly Macca into it? Just 'cause he's being two-timed.

Antony: She's not two-timing me, they're just mates.

Jim: She might not wanna be tied down. She might wanna play the field. Stick in there, son. You've got no qualifications, absolutely no prospects, but you never know – this other fella might be a right loser.

Antony: Right. That's it. I'm going to Darren's.

ANTONY GETS UP AND GOES. AWKWARD SILENCE FOR FORTY SECONDS OR SO.

Dave: What's up with him?

Barbara: What did you have to go and say that for, Jim? You know he's not got much confidence.

Jim: Well, she's taking him for a ride. I don't know why he's bloody bothering with her.

Denise: But you haven't even met her.

Jim: Well, I may as well tell him straight now, before he starts spending a load of money on her before she dumps him.

Barbara: That's all everything ever boils down to for you, Jim, innit? Money. That's all you ever think about.

Denise: Dad, you were dead tight on Antony then.

Jim: Who was singing 'Torn Between Two Bloody Lovers'?

Denise: As a *joke*. Poor Antony, he looked dead upset, didn't he? (PAUSE) Hey, Dave, what would you do if I went to the pictures with a fella who was just a friend?

Dave: Don't know.

Denise: But would you be mad?

Dave: Don't know.

Denise: You would though, wouldn't you?

Dave: I don't know.

Denise: You would.

Dave: I don't know, do I? You've not been, have you? And you're not gonna do, are you? Bloody 'ell.

Denise: Dave! Can't you try and be a bit more possessive? He's hopeless, him, isn't he?

Barbara: They're all the same, love. They're all over you until you marry 'em.

Denise: Yeah.

Barbara: Poor Antony.

PAUSE.

Dave: He really likes Emma, don't he?

Jim: (FEELING GUILTY) Oh, give over, will you – he's a young bloody lad. I'm not concerned about his lovelife – I'm more concerned about him getting a bloody job. That's what we should be worrying about. He's not tipping up enough, is he. It's wrong. The only bloody person who works in this house is your mother.

BIG PAUSE.

Barbara: Ooh Jim, Joe's got his date for the hospital. Oh, that's just broken my dream. I had a dream that Joe was pulling a caravan all on his own. Cheryl and Mary were inside and Joe was pulling it like a big shirehorse. I wonder what that means.

Jim: It means you're bloody mad. It's no wonder Joe's going into hospital pulling Cheryl and her mam about. Bloody 'ell, he must be knackered.

Barbara: Ooh, I was looking everywhere for Jim to go and help him.

Denise: D'you know what I keep dreaming about? Aeros and Twixes.

Jim: I've been having a weird one of them, you know. I keep dreaming that I'm strangling an old woman with an eye-patch.

Denise: Do you know who is a dead, dead heavy sleeper?

Barbara: Who?

Denise: Him. Dave, aren't you? Nothing wakes him.

Barbara: I can't sleep at night, me. He's asleep as soon as his head hits the pillow. He'd fall asleep on a washing line. Do you know Denise, last night I could hear your nana snoring in your old room, and your dad snoring next to me. (PAUSE) And the other night, your dad frightened me to death. He sat bolt upright in the middle of the night all of a sudden.

Denise: Was he dreaming?

Barbara: No, he thought he'd left the immersion on.

Denise (LAUGHS): You know when I'm alseep? Is the baby asleep as well do you think?

Barbara: Ooh.

Jim: No, it's awake more than that, love.

NANA GIVES A LITTLE SNORE.

Jim: Ey, Dave.

Dave: Yeah?

Jim: Can you bring the car round on Sunday to take Norma back, I mean, er, I don't like the idea of her on the bus with her eye-patch. It doesn't seem right.

Dave: Yeah, no bother. What time d'you want me round?

Barbara: Don't worry about it, Dave – to be honest I think she'll need to stay another week.

Jim: Another bloody week! Over my dead body.

Barbara: Jim! She thinks the world of you.

Jim: Thinks the bloody world of me?! Today, she had a family size bag of bloody Revels and did she offer me one? Did she shite. She sat there on her big fat arse announcing every one that she put in her big fat gob. 'Oh, coconut! Oh, orange! Oh, Malt-bloody-teaser . . .'

Barbara: Oh, is that it then? We can't look after my own mother because she wouldn't share a bag of Revels. Grow up, Jim.

Jim: *Me* grow up? She makes me un-bloody-plug everything at night before we go to bed – but she's got herself a bloody electric blanket on all night.

Barbara: Oooh, Jim. If it was your mam and dad, God rest their souls, I'd've done anything for 'em.

Jim: She should be in a bloody home.

Barbara: She is in a home. She's in *our* home. And that's where she's staying – with a family that loves her.

JIM SULKS.

Jim: (MUMBLES) 'Ooooh caramel, I think! No, wait, not caramel, coffee! Coffee one, that was . . .' Greedy old cow . . .

BIG PAUSE.

Nana: Is it nearly time for *The Bill*?

Jim: Hallo, Norma love. You're back with us, eh?

Nana: I wasn't alseep – I was just resting my eyes.

Jim: Course you were, love.

Nana: Ooh, hello, Denise.

Denise: Hiya, Nana.

Nana: Hello, David.

Dave: Hiya, Nana.

Nana: When did you come? I didn't hear you come.

Denise: Oh, we've not been here long. How're you feeling now, Nana?

Nana: Not so bad. It's very hard when you've got one eye, having been used to two. But I don't say anything. (PAUSE) What's that – I can't be doing with this. I don't watch this when I'm at home.

JIM LOOKS.

Jim: It's a good job you slept all the way through it then, eh, Norma?

Nana: Ooh, did you get my Sennapods, Barbara?

Barbara: Yeah.

NANA CROSSES HER FINGERS HOPEFULLY.

BIG PAUSE.

Nana: Do you know, Barbara, I think it might be a blockage.

Barbara: Do you?

Nana: Um. Something to do with my eye.

BIG PAUSE.

Nana: You know the specialist . . .

Barbara: Yeah.

Nana: Dr Crawford who operated on my eye. Do you know what he's called?

Barbara: Yeah. Mr Crawford.

Nana: Do you know what his name is? *Michael* Crawford. (LAUGHS) You know, like 'Oooh, Betty'. (LAUGHS) I didn't say anything to him, you know, because, well you can't to a specialist, can you, and I bet he gets it all the time.

PAUSE.

Nana: Hey, David, David. You'll like this. The specialist who operated on my eye. Do you know what he was called? *Michael* Crawford. You know, like 'Oooh, Betty'. You know, that programme . . . (LAUGHS) Oh, Denise, do you know what he said to me? Even though I'm taking the cataract out of your eye, I'm leaving the twinkle in. (LAUGHS) Oh, Barbara, I hope he has.

PAUSE.

Nana: Ooh, is it tonight? That thing with the man dressed as a chicken?

Barbara: Don't know, Mam.

Nana: You know, Denise? That man – he's a chicken. Ooh, it is funny. I do like that programme.

Denise: I don't know what you're on about, Nana.

Nana: David, will you look in the paper, I'd hate to miss it.

Dave: Do you know what it's called, Nana?

Nana: No.

Dave: I can't see anything it might be, Nana.

Nana: Oh, do you know what it was called, Barbara? That thing with a man dressed as a chicken . . .

Barbara: I don't know, Mam.

Jim: Right. That's it. Get your coat on, Dave.

END OF EPISODE FOUR.

Episode 5

JIM IS SITTING IN HIS CHAIR IN THE FRONT ROOM. THE DOORBELL RINGS.

Barbara: (SARCY) Don't worry about it, Jim, I'll get it.

JIM GIVES A 'WHAT HAVE I DONE NOW?' LOOK. HE FLICKS THE REMOTE CONTROL, AN ANNOYED LOOK ON HIS FACE. WE DON'T SEE BARBARA AND DENISE – THEY GO STRAIGHT TO THE KITCHEN. DAVE GREETS BARBARA AND COMES INTO THE LIVING ROOM.

Dave: All right, Barbara.

Denise: Hiya, Mam. Mam, what's up with ya? Mam?

Dave: All right, Jim.

Jim: Hiya, Dave.

Dave: What's up with Barbara, Jim? She looks a bit upset – Denise's gone in kitchen with her.

Jim: There's nothing wrong with her. It's the menopause. The bloody change – do you know what, I'm up to there with it.

CUT TO BARBARA AND DENISE IN THE KITCHEN:

Barbara: I'm just his bloody skivvy. It was worse when your nana was staying – I'd come home from work and that sink would be full of pots, they'd be fighting and I just wanted to get my coat on and go somewhere.

Denise: Aah, Mam. He is just so lazy.

Barbara: Well he hasn't got any hobbies. I try and think of things for him to do. He does the crossword in the paper right, so I bought him a *Puzzler* the other day and he just went mad, he said I'd wasted £1.70 and he wouldn't speak to me for the rest of the night. It's not a life this, it's just a bloody existence.

Denise: And he's always got bits of food stuck in his beard.

Barbara: Well he never has a wash.

CUT TO JIM AND DAVE IN THE FRONT ROOM:

Jim: How long does it last, this change malarky?

Dave: Dunno. Few years in't it?

Jim: Bloody 'ell.

CUT TO DENISE AND BARBARA IN THE KITCHEN:

Barbara: The only time he has a wash is when he goes to the doctor's. He just sits there mouthing off in that chair. Another time I came in, your nana's face was like thunder – he wouldn't put her drops in.

Denise: He is just so selfish.

Barbara: Poor Antony, got no confidence – Jim's knocked it all out of him, calling him a lanky streak of piss all the time.

Denise: Well, well he has got a point there.

CUT TO JIM AND DAVE IN THE FRONT ROOM:

Jim: Has *your* mum had her change yet?

Dave: Dunno – she's not said nowt.

CUT TO BARBARA AND DENISE IN THE KITCHEN:

Barbara: You know, most of the time, most of the time I put up with it – while you two were growing up.

Denise: Ah.

Barbara: Now I don't know why I'm here, Denise.

Denise: Ah, Mam, ah. You could come and live with us. No you could.

Barbara: Ah, Denise.

Denise: 'Cause when that baby's born I'm gonna be rushed off me feet. Ey.

CUT TO JIM AND DAVE IN THE FRONT ROOM:

Jim: Tell you what, Dave, you should have seen her before. She's gone too far this time.

Dave: Why?

Jim: Bang. She just switched the bloody telly off.

Dave: No need for that.

Jim: That's what I mean.

CUT TO KITCHEN:

Denise: Ah, ah. Do you like me new top?

CUT TO LIVING ROOM:

Jim: I'm not one of them husbands that goes out every night. Admittedly I would be if I could afford it. I have two nights and one afternoon a week and it's still not bloody good enough.

Dave: I don't wanna get involved me, Jim. She does work hard though.

Jim: Hard my arse. A couple of hours in a bloody bakery?

Dave: I don't wanna get involved. It's nowt to do with me.

CUT TO KITCHEN TO BARBARA CRYING AND THEN BACK TO FRONT ROOM:

Jim: The trouble with me lad, is I'm too easy-bloody-going. She walks all over me. I mean the days she does work in the bakery, it can be half seven, quarter to eight, before my tea's ready. But I don't say nothing, I just get on with it.

CUT TO KITCHEN:

Barbara: He's got no conversation about him at all. Do you know he absolutely hated work. Hated it. I always thought that when he gave it up, I'd see a lovely side of Jim that I'd never seen before. There isn't one.

Denise: No.

Barbara: You know the doctor said about this HRT thing. He said have a little think and go and discuss it with your husband. All Jim could say was that HRT's horse's piss and that them doctors are raking it in.

CUT TO LIVING ROOM: JIM AND DAVE ARE WATCHING TV.

DENISE COMES IN.

Episode 5   113

Denise: Ey, Dad, what've you said to me mam? Why d'you always have to upset her?

Jim: What?

Denise: You're horrible to her. You're always horrible to her and you're horrible to Nana 'n'all.

Jim: Bloody 'ell. What have I done now?

Denise: You never say anything nice to her. You never even offer to take her anywhere.

Jim: That's the bloody menopause that, isn't it. And anyway what about you? You're bloody lazier than me, aren't ya? I bet you still haven't cooked him a single meal since you've been married. Has she, Dave?

Denise: I have, haven't I, Dave?

Dave: Not a *meal*.

Denise: Oh shut it, you. (TO JIM) Anyway this is nothing to do with us. This is about you.

Jim: No it's about you, you and your bloody mother, 'cause she's poisoned your mind against me, hasn't she. And you're always on her bloody side. You're as thick as bloody thieves the pair of you. Why don't you just get your nana round here and the whole bloody coven can have a go at me. I tell you what Dave, you've made a hell of a mistake marrying into this lot, lad.

Denise: You don't deserve her, you.

Jim: She doesn't bloody deserve bloody me.

Denise: Dave! Why do you always take his side?

Dave: Well it's your mam's menopause in't it?

Jim: Cor-rect, David.

Denise: It's not her menopause, it's the way he treats her.

Dave: He's all right. Leave him alone.

Denise: Dave, will you keep your big fat nose out. It's nothing to do with you. It's not your family.

Dave: Well you've brought me in on this argument, haven't you. It's nothing to do with me. Bloody 'ell. Anyway what about you having a pop at your dad and you're never off your arse, are you?

Jim: Cor-rect, David.

Denise: I'm pregnant and I'm carrying your child about, thank you very much.

Dave: What d'you mean you're pregnant, you're carrying my child about thank you very much? Anyone'd think you were the only woman ever to bloody be pregnant. It's only the size of a bloody orange.

Denise: Well that's as much as you know – it's the size of a grapefruit, thank you, Dave.

Jim: Grapefruit my arse.

Dave: Cor-rect, Jim. (TO DENISE)

Jim: Thank you.

Dave: Anyway, how come we never go round to my mam and dad's?

Denise: Well, I'll tell you why, Dave – 'cause they sit on their arses and watch telly all night and it's boring. Anyway, you go round twice a week as it is.

Dave: That's to take me washing round and go back and pick it up again – you know that.

Denise: Oh well, well, well how come we've been married ages and your mum's never offered to do my washing.

Dave: Well you've got a washing machine, you should be doing my washing. Cost me two hundred and eighty notes that.

Jim: How much?

Dave: Two hundred and eighty bloody notes and she's never had a single thing in it.

Denise: Well you try being pregnant right and . . .

Dave: And what? And nothing. You're bone bloody idle.

Denise: I am preparing myself for motherhood.

Dave: Mother of my arse.

Jim: Cor-rect, Dave.

Dave: Thank you, James.

Jim: Who's 'em . . . Who's gonna wash the baby's things, Dave?

Denise: Will you stop shit-stirring it, Dad. It's nothing to do with you.

THEY HEAR THE FRONT DOOR SLAM. DENISE GOES TO THE WINDOW AND LOOKS OUT.

Denise: It's me mam. She's got her coat on. Dad, will you go after her?

Jim: Me, go after her? Why don't you go after her?

Denise: I'm pregnant! Dave, you go after her!

Dave: I'm watching this.

Jim: She's probably only gone to Mary's – to have a bloody go at me from round there. Anyway, Mary's the only one who doesn't know I'm a big, fat, lazy arse.

SILENCE. DENISE IS STILL AT THE WINDOW.

Denise: She's not gone to Mary's. I wonder where she's going? It's all your fault. She's on the change – she might walk out in front of a lorry and get run over.

Jim: Well, we could always put a claim in.

Denise: Poor Mam, I've never seen her so upset. You're horrible, you. You've broke our home up.

Jim: It's not even your bloody home, you don't live here.

Denise: Mam said Antony stormed out. Now she's gone. I'll be next.

Jim: You're too bloody lazy to storm off anywhere, you.

Denise: No, *you're* the lazy one.

Jim: *You're* the bloody lazy one.

Denise: Get lost – you're way lazier than me.

PAUSE.

Jim: My arse. You are.

Denise: No *you* are.

Jim: (TO DAVE) *She* is.

Denise: (TO DAVE) *He* is.

JIM TURNS OVER. *WHO WANTS TO BE A MILLIONAIRE?* IS ON. HE RUBS HIS HANDS IN GLEE.

All: Waaay.

Jim: I tell you what, this is got to be the best bloody show on the television, bar none.

Dave: (RUBS HANDS TOGETHER) Too right.

THEY WATCH *WHO WANTS TO BE A MILLIONAIRE?* THE QUESTION IS ABOUT FABRIC AND NATIONALITIES.

Jim: Persian! Bloody Persian. Persian man and Persian rug.

Dave: I guess B. Jute. Oh, yes.

Denise: Clever dick. Got that wrong didn't you.

Dave: Dave Best got it right.

CHRIS TARRANT ANNOUNCES ARLENE FROM ABERDEENSHIRE.

Jim: Come on, Arlene. Come on, love.

Dave: (TO TUNE OF 'COME ON EILEEN', SINGS) Come on, Arlene . . .

CHRIS TARRANT ASKS, 'WHAT WOULD YOU DO IF YOU WON £1M?'

Denise: (OF ARLENE) Get her roots done.

QUESTION ABOUT BONES.

Jim: Skeleton!

Denise: Oh, em?

Dave: B: Skeleton.

Jim: Yes, a hundred pound. A piece of piss.

ECOLOGICAL GROUP QUESTION. 'GREEN' IS THE ANSWER.

Jim: No. No. No. Yes.

Dave: D: Green.

Jim: Two hundred notes. Piss easy.

HARDEST SUBSTANCE QUESTION.

Jim: Duckers.

DAVE KILLS HIMSELF LAUGHING. ARLENE ANSWERS A QUESTION ON PIRATES.

Dave: Duckers (PAUSE) Ooh, yes.

Denise: You'd think she'd put a bit more lippy on wouldn't you, you know, going on telly?

Dave: Yeah, well she's nervous, she keeps on licking it off. Look.

Denise: Oh yeah.

Dave: Watch. Look.

GOLF QUESTION. DENISE LAUGHS.

Denise: Bogey. Dave, Dave, bogey. Dad, do you know what Dave calls crows, bogeys.

QUESTION ABOUT THE SONG 'LIFTED'.

Dave: Lighthouse Family. Number one, August 1995. Got everything they've ever done. C: Lighthouse Family. Correct love. Come on, Chris.

Denise: Hey, Dave.

Dave: Got everything they've ever done.

Denise: Dad, Dave.

QUESTION ABOUT HIND.

Jim: Horse's arse. Horse's arse. Horse's arse. Horse's arse.

Denise: It was a deer.

Jim: Looks like a horse's arse from the back.

ETHANOL QUESTION.

Dave: Ethanol?

Denise: Most common form . . .

Jim: Substance?

Denise: Phone a friend.

Dave: Phone a friend.

Jim: Say if one of us was on the show and we had to phone your nana. She'd spend the first half hour telling us about where she fell in the precinct.

PAUSE.

ARLENE PHONES HER SISTER.

Denise: She's phoning her sister.

Dave: Gotta be one of them four.

Denise: Yeah. Ah, her bottle's gone, innit.

Jim: She doesn't know.

Dave: Tell you what, her bottle's gone.

Denise: Ah he'd love her to win, Chris, 'n'all.

Dave: Tell you summit, he'd love her to win, Chris.

Denise: Fifty-fifty. Fifty-fifty.

Dave: Going fifty-fifty.

THE ANSWER IS ALCOHOL. ARLENE LOSES, BUT SAYS 'OK, COOL'.

Dave: Alcohol. I'd've thought you'd know that, Denise.

Denise: I've never even drank ethanol!

PAUSE.

Denise: Aah, she looks dead upset, Dad, doesn't she?

ARLENE'S WON £1000.

Jim: She still won a grand though, didn't she.

Dave: Oh yeah. Gutted though, in't she?

Jim: Yeah.

CHRIS TARRANT SAYS 'NINE OF YOU LEFT'.

Jim: That'll be nine arses going at the same time there, Dave.

PAUSE.

Jim: Ey, nine little bottoms chewing on their undies. Oh ey, tell you what, I came close to winning the lottery on Saturday.

Dave: Did you?

Jim: One bloody number I wanted, number 17 and 18 popped out. I was that bloody close, ey, that close to winning a tenner.

Denise: Ey, Dad, what was that other quiz show that you used to really like? With, em, oh what's his name, thingy? Er, Roy Walker.

Jim: Oh, *Catchphrase*.

PAUSE. THEY WATCH TELLY.

Dave: 'Say what you see, if you see it, say it.'

PAUSE.

Jim: 'It's a good answer, but it's not right.'

Dave: 'Say what you see, if you see it, say it.' 'Say what you see, if you see it, say it.' 'Say what you see, if you see it, say it.'

PAUSE.

Denise: Dave, stop it.

Dave: I'm only saying what I see.

Denise: But you're not seeing it, so stop saying it.

Jim: Do y'know who the best quiz master is, Dave?

Dave: Les Dennis.

Jim: Ugh, ugh. Bob Monkhouse.

Dave: Ugh, ugh.

Jim: Ugh, ugh.

Dave: Ugh, ugh.

Jim: Ugh, ugh. Eh, what about old Brucie baby?

Dave: Good game, good game. Nice to see you, to see you nice. Here they are, they're so appealing, okay dollies, do your dealing!

Jim: Higher than an eight. Higher than an eight. Lower. Lower.

LAUGH.

Dave: Eh, remember him, remember him? Ooh look at the muck here, ooh Everhard. Shut that door.

Jim: Dave, don't do that.

THE FRONT DOOR CLOSES.

Jim: Ugh, ugh.

THEY ALL WATCH THE DOOR. BARBARA COMES IN AND SITS DOWN, RESIGNED. DENISE HANDS MAM AN ASHTRAY.

Barbara: Ta. (DENISE HANDS HER A CIGGY) Ta.

Denise: You all right, Mam?

Barbara: Yeah.

Dave: You all right, Barbara?

Barbara: Yeah.

Jim: You're all right, Barb?

Barbara: I have to be, don't I?

Jim: I've walked the length of this neighbourhood looking for you. You've had us worried out of our bloody minds here.

Denise: Where did you go, Mam?

Barbara: I just went for a little walk – to clear me head.

Denise: Anything the matter, Mam?

Barbara: No nothing. Nothing that won't keep. I've kept it in for over twenty-seven years now.

Jim: I'll tell you what, Barb, there was a woman just like you, on the change. She made a thousand pounds there on the telly. So it's not all doom and gloom. Look, you and your change, you just sit there and I'll make us a nice cup of tea.

THEY ALL LOOK AT JIM IN DISBELIEF.

Jim: Nice cup of tea, Barb? (SHE IGNORES HIM) Nice cup of tea, Dave? Denise? Nice cup of tea for you and the little one? Medium to strong, eh? I'll go and heat the pot and we'll let it brew, eh. There's a nice cup of tea coming your way. A nice cup of tea coming your way. Oh and keep an eye on Dave from Halifax for me because *I am making a brew*. Even though it's my favourite programme, *I am making a brew*. And do you know why? Because *I am a family man*.

DAVE SMILES. DENISE AND BARBARA ARE TRYING NOT TO SMILE.

Jim: Barbara, if you would like some conversation with me about Pauline or Donna or just a bakery chit-chat, think on while I'm making the brew.

HE GETS UP AND GOES TO THE KITCHEN. THE CAMERA STAYS IN THE LIVING ROOM. DENISE LOOKS AT BARBARA, BARBARA SHAKES HER HEAD.

CUT TO JIM: STANDING IN THE KITCHEN DOORWAY, WATCHING *WHO WANTS TO BE A MILLIONAIRE?*

Jim: D! Kent. Kettle's nearly boiling love, nice and hot, 'cause when you're making tea, the water's gotta be really piping.

JIM GOES BACK INTO THE KITCHEN.

Jim (OOV): We'll have to get a portable in here, Barb. Sugar bowl's empty, Barb, where's the sugar?

Barbara: Top left-hand cupboard, where it always is.

BIG PAUSE.

Jim: Any biscuits, Barb?

Barbara: There's some Penguins in the big Tupperware box.

BIG PAUSE.

Jim: Where is the Tupperware box?

Barbara: In the cupboard with the cornflakes.

BIG PAUSE.

Jim: There's no Penguins, Barb.

Barbara: Oooh. (SHE GOES TO THE KITCHEN WHERE JIM IS MAKING THE BREW. SHE PLONKS THEM ON TO THE TRAY) 'Ere. (SHE GOES TO LEAVE).

Jim: Ey, Barb? We'll get through this change thing together, you know what I mean, kid?

Barbara: Yeah.

PAUSE.

Jim: Making a little brew. Making a lovely pot of tea here. (BARBARA GOES. HE WHISTLES 'TEA FOR TWO', THEN, TO HIMSELF) 'D'you know the piano's on my foot?' 'You hum, sir, and I'll play it.' 'You hum it and I'll play it.'

JIM GOES BACK INTO LIVING ROOM AND HANDS OUT THE TEAS.

Jim: Nice cup of tea, David.

Dave: Thank you, James.

Barbara: Thanks, Jim.

Jim: There y'are, for the grapefruit.

Denise: Thank you.

Jim: Ooh, nectar. Who wants to be a millionaire? I bloody don't. I'm already a millionaire – with a million pound of love in the bank. Dave? You having that, Dave?

Dave: Good one that, James.

Jim: And I tell you what, tomorrow night, I'd like to cordially invite you round to my simple, modest home – that's Dave and Denise and the grapefruit, to join me and my lovely wife, Barbara, who will come home from work to find me entertaining her sweet-smelling mother whilst preparing a meal.

Denise: You're not gonna cook? Are you gonna cook?

Jim: My onion gravy, a delicacy, will be gently caressing the fluffy mash which will be straddled by two succulent sausages. Ey? (RUBS HIS HANDS) How does that grab you, Barb? (HE KISSES HIS FINGERS) Okay, Dave?

Barbara: Well I'll believe it when I see it.

PAUSE. JIM SLURPS HIS TEA.

Dave: Ey, hang on. Tomorrow night? That's the darts final in the Feathers, Jim.

Jim: Oh bloody 'ell, yeah, I forgot all about that. Ah well, the thought was there, Barb. (THEY ALL LOOK AT HIM). What?

END OF EPISODE FIVE.

Episode 6

BARBARA IS FUSSING ABOUT THE ROOM. JIM WATCHES *EASTENDERS*.

Jim: Mike Reid – he must pinch himself every bloody morning, him. I bet you he can't believe his own bloody luck. He used to be a comedian, you know, Mike Reid. 'Stitch that. Wallop.'

Barbara: Switch it off, Jim. They'll be here soon.

JIM DOESN'T MOVE.

Jim: Ah, I'll just watch that, Barb.

Barbara: You're always slagging it!

Jim: She's still got a fine pair, ol' Barbara Windsor, hasn't she, I'll give her that.

Barbara: Ey, Jim, d'you think we've got enough lagers? I hope we have. Will you nip out for some if we haven't?

Jim: What with?

DOORBELL GOES.

Jim: There's the door, Barb.

Barbara: Oh, hiya Twiggy. Are you all right? It's Twiggy.

Twiggy: You all right, Barb?

Barbara: Yeah.

BARBARA AND TWIGGY COME INTO THE LIVING ROOM.

Jim: All right, Twigg?

Twiggy: You all right, Jim?

Barbara: Have you got that sovereign ring, Twiggy?

Twiggy: Have I ever let you down, Barb? There y'are, girl.

Barbara: Ta. Oh, it's lovely. Look Jim.

Jim: Nice one.

Barbara: I'd better get it wrapped up.

BARBARA STARTS WRAPPING IT.

Jim: How much do we owe you for the ring, Twigg?

Twiggy: Twenty notes.

Jim: How much did *you* pay for it?

Twiggy: Twenty notes. Ey, I don't rip off me mates, you know.

Jim: Go 'way, you'd flog your own grandmother, you would Twigg.

Twiggy: Ey, Barb, that looks like a nice buffet.

Barbara: Oh, don't start it now.

Twiggy: Where is he – the birthday boy?

Barbara: He's round at Emma's – but he'll be back in a minute.

Barbara: Oh ey, Twiggy. You should've brought your girlfriend.

Twiggy: No, I'm not seeing her now.

Barbara: Aaaah. Are you not?

Twiggy: Well, she was a bit of bike really.

Jim: Well, I thought that's why you liked her.

Twiggy: Yeah – but you don't want everyone else having a go on it, d'you know what I mean?

Barbara: It's a shame that, Twiggy – she was handy for you wasn't she at that petrol station.

Twiggy: Yeah. I put up a load of shelves for her, you know, bought her a gold ankle chain *and* grouted her bathroom. Turns out she's knocking off Duckers 'n'all.

Barbara: Oh what? I am sorry. How did you find out?

Twiggy: Duckers told me.

Barbara: Did he?

Twiggy: Well he *is* me mate, isn't he?

Barbara: Oh yeah . . .

Twiggy: To be quite honest, I didn't want to get lumbered with all them kids.

Barbara: Well, I didn't like to say anything at the time, Twiggy, but I did think she was a bit common. You can do a lot better than that.

Twiggy: Yeah. Mind you, so can Duckers.

Barbara: Yeah. Ey, how's your little lad, Lee? You should've brought him, couldn't you?

Twiggy: Well, she's gone on off on one – won't let me see him just because I got bladdered when I was supposed to have access. You know what she's like. The only time I can speak to him now is on his mobile.

PAUSE.

TWIGGY AND JIM WATCH TV.

Twiggy: (OF *EASTENDERS*) Ey! 'Wallop.' (PAUSE) Tell you what, Jim, he is one lucky bleeder him, landing that job.

Barbara: Are you going to get changed for the party, Jim?

Jim: Why? I'm all right like this, aren't I? Party? Come on, party my arse. You've only made a few butties haven't you, and that's only because you want a look at Emma.

BARBARA HANDS JIM SOME BALLOONS.

Barbara: Will you blow those balloons up for me, Jim?

Jim: He's eighteen, Barb, not bloody eight.

Barbara: Well, will you blow them up then, Twiggy?

Twiggy: Yeah, yeah, no danger.

Jim: When I was eighteen my old man took me for a bevvy and that was it.

Barbara: Jim, they're only a few balloons. We had 'em for Denise, so we're gonna have to have 'em for our Antony.

Jim: Balloons my arse. Pass 'em over, will you. Twigg, pass them here. Tell you what, you never get a bloody minute to yourself in this house.

TWIGGY AND JIM BLOW UP THE BALLOONS IN SILENCE. BARBARA GOES OFF TO THE KITCHEN.

Jim: I could do with a pair of bellows up my arse.

PAUSE.

Twiggy: (HOLDS A ROUND BALLOON AT HIS BREAST) Ey, Jim, what does that remind you of?

THEY BOTH LAUGH CHILDISHLY.

Jim: Beverly Macca.

Twiggy: Correct.

JIM PLACES A LONG BALLOON AT HIS CROTCH.

Jim: Twiggy, what about this one. Oh nurse, what time's my operation?

THEY CONTINUE BLOWING UP BALLOONS. JIM PASSES A BALLOON TO TWIGGY TO TIE UP.

Jim: Here you are, Twigg. Do that. I tell you what, it takes it out of you this, doesn't it?

Twiggy: (HANGS A LONG ONE WITH TWO ROUND ONES EITHER SIDE) Ey, Jim.

Jim: (OF RUDE BALLOONS) Leave that like that. It'll bloody annoy Norma.

Twiggy: Is she coming?

Jim: Oh yeah. She's off tonight – it's not Hallowe'en is it?

TWIGGY AND JIM CONTINUE TO BLOW BALLOONS.

Twiggy: So your Antony's bringing his bird, eh?

Jim: Oh aye, it'll only last five minutes. She'll soon suss out the lazy-arse sod.

Twiggy: Eh, d'you remember Denise's eighteenth? That went off big style didn't it?

Jim: That was great.

DOORBELL GOES.

Jim: Barbara! 'Ere y'are Twigg.

BALLOON FLIES OFF.

Twiggy: Oh, you're bleeding useless, you are, Jim.

Barbara (OOV): Oh, hiya, Darren. Come in. You all right? It's Darren.

Twiggy: Hello, Darren. How's it going?

Darren: All right, thanks.

Barbara: Would you like a lager, Darren?

Darren: Oh, yeah please.

Barbara: Ah. Sit down.

Jim: All right, Darren? What d'you know, lad?

Darren: Nowt really.

Jim: When's your court case?

Darren: A week on Thursday.

Jim: You'll be all right won't you. Is it your first offence?

Darren: No.

Jim: What d'you think of your chances?

Darren: Dunno really.

Jim: Have you got a good solicitor?

Darren: No.

BIG PAUSE

DOORBELL GOES.

Jim: Get that will you, Barb. (PAUSE) You don't get a bloody minute in this house.

Barbara (OOV): Hello, Mam.

Nana (OOV): Hello, Barbara.

Denise (OOV): Hiya, Mam.

Barbara (OOV): Denise, you look lovely.

Denise: You look lovely, Mam.

Barbara: Hello, Dave. You look lovely.

DENISE, DAVE AND NANA WALK IN, FOLLOWED BY BARBARA.

Jim: Hello, Norma. How nice to see you again.

Twiggy: 'Ere y'are, love. Sit here, love.

THEY MOVE THE BALLOONS.

Denise: Hiya, Dad.

Jim: Hello, love.

Dave: All right, Darren?

Jim: All right, Dave?

Dave: Hiya, Jim. Yeah.

Denise: Is Antony not here?

Jim: Not yet.

Nana: (TO DARREN) Which one are you?

Barbara: This is Darren, Mam. Would you like a drink, Dave?

Dave: I'll have lager please, Barbara.

Barbara: Denise?

Denise: Anything, ta.

Barbara: Mam, would you like a drink?

Nana: No, I'd better not. Go on then. I'll have a sherry, love.

Denise: Has nobody got no music on or nowt?

Jim: It's broke. Don't worry. I'll get the banjo out in a minute.

Barbara: Oh, leave off that thing, Jim! We don't want Emma thinking we're the Beverly Hillbillies.

Dave: 'Deliverance', you mean.

JIM LAUGHS AND SINGS THE TUNE. BARBARA PASSES NANA A DRINK.

Barbara: Here y'are, Mam.

Nana: Oh ta, love.

Barbara: How are you Denise? Had a nice day?

Denise: Yeah.

Dave: She's spent most of it doing her hair.

Denise: It is a party, Dave.

Barbara: It's a party, Dave. (PAUSE) Oooh, Darren, is your mam all right?

Darren: Yeah.

Barbara: I heard she was in hospital.

Darren: Oh yeah – she is, yeah.

Barbara: Ah, your poor mam. What's up with her?

Darren: I'm not quite sure really.

Barbara: Oooh, do they not know what it is then?

Darren: I dunno.

Barbara: Aaah, give her my love won't you?

Darren: Yeah.

JIM WATCHES BARBARA PUTTING UP DECORATIONS.

Jim: Are you keeping that straight, Barb?

Barbara: Oh, Jim, put your shoes on. We don't want a whiff of 'em feet.

Denise: They smell like Stilton, them. And 'ey, Dad, when Emma's here, if you go for a wee, shut the toilet door.

Barbara: And don't pick your arse.

Jim: Bloody 'ell, I may as well just go and sit in the bleedin' shed.

DARREN LAUGHS.

DOOR GOES.

Jim: Get that door, Barb.

Denise: That'll be Antony with Emma.

ANTONY AND EMMA ARRIVE.

Barbara: Hello, love. Hello, Emma.

DAVE, DENISE, JIM, BARBARA, TWIGGY AND NANA ALL SING THE WHOLE OF 'HAPPY BIRTHDAY'.

Barbara: (KISSES ANTONY) Happy Birthday.

Antony: This is Emma.

Denise: Oooh.

Barbara: We're very pleased to meet you Emma. We've heard a lot about you. Oh, you don't know who everyone is, do you. That's Denise – she's Antony's sister.

Denise: Hiya.

Emma: Hiya.

Barbara: And this is David – Antony's sister's husband.

Jim: Bloody 'ell, Barb, it's not *This Is Your Life*.

Barbara: Oh, shut up, Jim. That's Jim – Antony's father.

Emma: Hello, Mr Royle.

Barbara: You know Darren, don't you?

Emma: Yeah, you all right Darren?

Darren: All right.

Barbara: This is Nana.

Nana: Hello, love.

Emma: Hello.

Barbara: And there's Twiggy.

Emma: Right.

Jim: Sit yourself down, love.

Barbara: Ooh, I'll get you a chair.

JIM HANDS ANTONY THE PRESENT.

Jim: There y'go, Lurch.

Antony: Sound.

ANTONY OPENS IT – IT'S A SOVEREIGN RING.

Darren: That's well smart. Nice one.

Antony: Look at that, ey?

ANTONY PUTS IT ON.

Nana: Oh, it does suit you, Antony.

Antony: (TO DARREN. MOCK *FAST SHOW* CHARACTERS) Suits you, sir.

Darren: Suits you, sir. D'you want it, sir?

Antony: Do you, sir?

Darren: Do you want it, sir? Do you?

Nana: Course he wants it – it's his birthday present.

Dave: D'you know Patrick who owns Jazzbo's? He's got three of them sovereigns on his hand in a row there. (HOLDS HIS FINGERS UP) See there? Looks top.

Barbara: Oooh, Emma, would you like a drink?

Emma: Erm, well, I'm driving – so just an orange please.

Barbara: Oh, I don't think I've got any orange. Would you like some Vimto?

Emma: Er, I'm all right thanks.

Barbara: Help yourself to the buffet. Can I get you a ham sandwich?

Emma: Oh, no thank you, I'm a vegetarian.

Barbara: Ooh, can I do you a Dairylea instead?

Emma: No, honestly, I'm fine thank you.

Barbara: She can have Dairylea, can't she, Denise?

Denise: Yeah.

Nana: What is she?

Denise: She's a vegetarian, Nana.

Nana: Oooh, you could have a bit of cheese though. Have you got some cheese, Barbara? Oh, Emma, it's a shame for you.

Jim: Look, if she doesn't want anything, she doesn't want any. Leave the girl alone.

Antony: She's all right.

Jim: That's a belting little car that, love. What does your Dad drive?

Nana: Could you have some wafer-thin ham? Could she have wafer-thin ham, Barbara?

Barbara: No.

Nana: Ooh, do you know, we've heard nothing from Antony but Emma, Emma, Emma. It's the first time I've known Antony courting.

Denise: Nana, don't be saying that.

Nana: Is your nana still alive, Emma?

Emma: Yeah.

Nana: Does she live with you?

Emma: No.

Nana: Emma, Emma, I've had my cataracts done. And if you'd've come here two weeks ago, I wouldn't have been able to see you.

Emma: Why?

Nana: Because I had this patch on my eye. It's a very serious operation. But I don't say anything. I was very well looked after here – I didn't want to go home.

Jim What did you say your dad's motor was, love?

Emma: A BMW.

Antony: I thought he had that four-wheel drive.

Emma: No, that's my mum's.

JIM RUBS HIS FINGERS TOGETHER AND MOUTHS 'TWO CARS' TO DAVE.

PAUSE.

Barbara: I'll get a little drink.

Dave: Did you know that Denise was pregnant?

Emma: No, I didn't.

Dave: Yeah, we're having a baby.

Emma: Yeah? Congratulations.

Denise: Aah. Thanks, Emma. Mam! Antony's never even told Emma that I'm pregnant.

Barbara: Oh.

Nana: She didn't know about my cataracts either.

Barbara: Antony, get Emma a Wagon Wheel.

ANTONY GOES TO THE KITCHEN.

Denise: I can smell something in here.

Barbara: I've told him to put his shoes on.

Jim: It's not me.

Denise: Can you smell it?

Barbara: Ooh, that smells like dog muck.

Nana: 'Muck for luck!'

Barbara: Who's brought that in? Is that you, Darren?

Darren: Don't know.

Barbara: Well have a look. Somebody's walked it in.

EVERYONE LOOKS AT THEIR SHOES.

Barbara: Is there anything there, Jim?

Jim: No.

Dave: Oh no – I think it's me. Sorry, Emma.

Emma: You're all right.

Denise: Dave! Take it off, you big clown. Oh, I'm so sorry Emma.

Dave: I'll leave it on to dry, then it'll be easier to get off.

Denise: Oh, Mam, will you get his shoe off him.

Nana: 'Muck for luck.'

Antony: Sorry, Emma.

Dave: Sorry, Emma.

Barbara: What a thing to happen. I am sorry, Emma.

Emma: It's all right.

Barbara: I bet this never happens at your house, does it?

Nana: (TO DARREN) Is your nana still alive, Gary?

Denise: Nana, it's Darren.

Darren: Yeah.

Nana: Does she live with you, Darren?

Darren: No.

Jim: Oh well, I'll have to nip upstairs. I've got a turtle's head in me underpants.

DARREN LAUGHS.

Denise: Dad!

JIM GOES UP TO THE LOO.

BARBARA IS IN THE KITCHEN, WASHING DAVE'S SHOE AT THE SINK. MARY, JOE AND CHERYL COME IN THE BACK DOOR.

Mary: Only us!

Barbara: Hiya, Mary. Hiya, Cheryl. Oh, you look nice. Hello, Joe.

Joe: Hello, Barbara.

JOE AND CHERYL GO THROUGH TO THE LIVING ROOM.

MARY STAYS IN THE KITCHEN WITH BARBARA.

Mary: Is Emma here?

Barbara: Oh, yes.

Mary: What's she like?

Barbara: She's a really lovely girl – she's a vegetarian though.

Mary: Ah well, it's happened to a lot of them.

Barbara: Yeah, ooh, I'm trying to get this off Dave's shoe.

Mary: Dog dirt.

Barbara: Yeah. (PAUSE) Do you know, Mary, I've had a whole day of it today – Jim's been so miserable, and now this has happened.

Mary: I know, but isn't it a good job that we can laugh at it?

Barbara: Oh, yeah.

Mary: Oh, er, did you notice anything funny about Joe? I think he's a bit drunk.

Barbara: Ooh.

Mary: He was at a bowling club do.

Barbara: Oh, ho ho.

Mary: Oh, we've put a tenner in Antony's card.

Barbara: Aah. Oh Mary, you shouldn't have.

Mary: So hard to know what to get them.

Barbara: Oh yeah. Well, they're not babies anymore.

Mary: I know. Isn't it awful? They're all grown up. My Cheryl's the same.

Barbara: Mary, will you do me a little favour? When you go in there, will you have a little smell round for me. Tell me if you can still smell anything untoward.

Mary: I will Barbara. I'm a great one for smelling anything.

Barbara: Oh, thanks Mary.

ANTONY IS UNWRAPPING CHERYL'S PRESENT. IT'S A STEREOPHONICS CD.

Twiggy: Pies are great, Dave.

Antony: Cheers, Cheryl.

Twiggy: Where did you get that, Cheryl? I can get you anything like that, you know.

Cheryl: Now you tell me.

Twiggy: Have you got enough there, Dave?

Dave: Well, she's not done me any tea, has she?

Joe: Ey, Darren, Darren . . . er . . . I want to tell you something. I saw Bob Carter – I haven't seen him for fifteen years and I saw him today. He grew up on our street, then he moved . . . Bury way, I think it was. I haven't seen him for fifteen years and, bugger me, he turned up at the bowling club.

Darren: Very good, Joe.

Barbara: (RETURNING WITH DAVE'S SHOE) Dave – nice and clean.

Dave: Thanks, Barbara.

Barbara: Mam, do you want something to eat?

Nana: Can I have something to drink, love, please and just a bit to eat.

Barbara: All right. Not a lot. Okay.

Nana: Have you got something cheesey?

Barbara: Oh, I have.

Mary: (TO TWIGGY) Don't be giving Joe any more drink, he's had enough.

Twiggy: Has he heck.

Mary: Ooh, happy birthday, Antony – and this must be Emma.

Emma: Hiya.

Mary: Aah, so many new names for you! Just remember we're Mary and Joseph – like in the Bible. But we've got Cheryl, not Jesus.

Joe: Image of his brother. Had his leg taken off in the Sixties, his brother.

Barbara: Ooh.

Joe: Hell of a nice fella though. Never bothered him about his leg.

Barbara: Aah. Didn't it?

PASSES DRINK TO MARY.

Mary: Thanks, love.

Barbara: Here y'are, Mam.

JIM COMES BACK DOWN PLAYING THE BANJO.

Everyone: Waaaaay!

JIM STRIKES ROCK STAR POSE.

Barbara: No, no, we're going to have a toast. Come and sit down.

Nana: You made me jump.

BARBARA HANDS TWIGGY THE BOTTLE TO OPEN, HE OPENS IT THEN PASSES IT BACK. BIG CHEER AS BARBARA POURS THE POMAGNE. MARY HELPS HER HAND IT OUT

Barbara: Jim, are you going to say something?

Jim: Yeah.

Dave: Turn the volume down on the telly, Jim.

Jim: The telly's going for a burton.

Twiggy: Here you go lads. (HANDS IT TO ANTONY AND DARREN).

Jim: Ladies and gentlemen, I'd just like to say how lucky we are

that our Antony's been able to get a few hours off work today –
oh, I've just remembered, Barb, he's not working, is he. Anyway,
Antony, you've come of age, so you can have your first legal
drop of ale, eh, young man. Anyway, he's not a bad lad really so
. . . I'd like to propose a toast: to Antony James Royle – my son
and heir to the whole of this estate. Happy eighteenth birthday,
Lurchio.

Denise/Dave/Barbara/Jim/Twiggy: Waaaay! Speech Antony.

Antony: What?

Barbara: Say something.

Antony: I haven't got owt to say really.

Jim: Well, I'd like to say a nice big thank you to Emma for
putting to one side all our doubts about our Antony being a
sausage jockey.

Barbara: Oooh, Jim. Oh Mary, in't he awful? Ignore him, Emma.
Happy birthday, Antony.

Denise/Jim/All: Happy birthday, Antony.

Dave: Waaay! (SINGS, EVERYONE JOINS IN) For he's a jolly
good fellow, for he's a jolly good fellow, for he's a jolly good
fellow, and so say all of us.

All: Speech.

Denise: Go on, Antony – say something.

Antony: I told you, I've got nowt to say.

Denise: He's a right gawp.

Dave: Come on, you've got to say something.

Antony: I'd just like to say thanks to everyone for coming. Er . . . thanks.

Jim: Did you help him to write that speech, Darren?

Darren: No.

Mary: Do you remember, Antony, when you were a little boy and you used to come in wanting ten p from me? And then you used to do the 'Birdy Song' for me and Joe?

EVERYONE LAUGHS AND STARTS DOING THE 'BIRDY SONG'. THEN, JIM PLAYS ONE SONG ON THE BANJO.

Jim: Now in the family,
        we have an heirloom,
        handed down to me some years ago,
        it may be half a century since Grandad
        was a lad,
        I'll tell you what it is
        and then you'll know.
        Well, it's my grandad's flannelette nightie,
        and I was christened one day,
        at the church they were in a whirl,
        'cos no one seemed to know
        if I'm a boy or a girl,
        because they'd had one or two
        and they were in a mess,
        that's all they'd tell the preacher.
        He said, 'I even had a quiz,
        to find out what he is,
        by his Grandad's flannelette shirt.'

Everyone at the end: 'Waaaay'.

JOE, FROM HIS SEAT AT THE TABLE, NEXT TO THE BUFFET,

STARTS SINGING. THE CAMERA PANS THE ROOM
THROUGHOUT.

Joe: I'll take you home again Kathleen,
Across the ocean wild and wide . . .

Nana: (OVER THE SINGING, HOLDS HANDS UP TO
SILENCE EVERYONE, EYES SHUT) Oooh, I love this one . . .

Joe: To where your heart has ever been
Since first you were my bonny bride.
The roses all have left your cheek,
I've watched them fade away and die,
Your voice is sad when e'er you speak,
And tears bedim your loving eyes.

(REFRAIN):
Oh! I will take you back, Kathleen,
To where your heart will feel no pain.
And when the fields are fresh and green,
I'll take you to your home again.

I know you love me, Kathleen dear,
Your heart is ever fond and true.
I always feel when you are near,
That life holds nothing dear, but you.

The smiles that once you gave to me,
I scarcely ever see them now
Though many, many times I see
A dark'ning shadow on your brow.

(REFRAIN)

Nana: (CRYING) Your dad used to sing this . . .

Joe: To that dear home beyond the sea,
My Kathleen shall again return.
And when thy old friends welcome thee,
Thy loving heart will cease to yearn

Where laughs the little silver stream,
Beside your mother's humble cot
And brightest rays of sunshine gleam
There all your grief will be forgot.

(REFRAIN)

SLIGHT PAUSE AT THE END OF THE SONG.

Darren: I can still smell shit in here.

END OF EPISODE SIX.

The Royle Family at Christmas

Episode 7

CAMERA PULLS OUT FROM DANCING MEDIEVAL MINSTRELS ON *NOEL'S CHRISTMAS PRESENTS*. IT PANS ROUND TO JIM, SPORTING PAPER HAT (CROWN), CHRISTMAS CARDIGAN AND A LOOK OF DISDAIN.

MOVE TO NANA – WHO'S ASLEEP (WITH HAT) – THEN DAVE AND ANTONY WHO ARE BOTH WATCHING TELLY.

SILENCE FOR THE WHOLE PAN ROUND.

CAMERA GOES TO KITCHEN WHERE BARBARA (COMPLETE WITH PAPER HAT) IS ELBOW-DEEP IN WASHING-UP. A BIG TURKEY CARCASS SITS IN THE MIDDLE OF THE KITCHEN TABLE.

JIM, BARBARA AND NANA WEAR THEIR CHRISTMAS PAPER HATS THROUGHOUT THE WHOLE EPISODE.

THE PHONE (IN THE KITCHEN) GOES.

Barbara: Hello. Aah. Hiya, love. How are you feeling, Denise? Aah. Aah. Oh . . . well, your nana's asleep, your dad's being miserable and Antony and Dave are watching Noel Edmonds. Yeah. Yeah. Oh. So are you feeling better then? Aah, yeah. . . . Yeah. Are you coming down then?

CUT TO BEDROOM WHERE DENISE IS LYING ON THE BED, ON A MOBILE PHONE. WE ONLY SEE HER HEAD AND SHOULDERS.

Denise: Yeah, I think I will. Hey, in't it great Dave got me this mobile phone?

Barbara: Yeah. Aah. Should I come up and get ya?

Denise: No, I'll be all right. Bye.

CAMERA PANS OUT, REVEALING DENISE'S BUMP. WITH GREAT EFFORT SHE GETS OFF THE BED.

BARBARA GOES INTO THE LIVING ROOM.

Barbara: Hey, Dave, it's great that mobile you've bought for our Denise. It's dead handy. She's just phoned me from upstairs.

Dave: That's supposed to be for emergencies, when the baby's born. Bloody 'ell, they're not cheap them.

Jim: How much are they, Dave?

Dave: Forty notes.

Jim: Bloody 'ell.

DENISE WALKS IN AND SITS DOWN.

Dave: Y'all right.

Denise: Yeah.

Dave: Had a nice sleep?

Denise: Yeah. Hey, Dave, I really love that mobile what you got me.

Dave: Hey, you're not supposed to be using it though, not from upstairs.

Denise: I've only rang me mam on it!

Jim: I bet you them calls are not cheap either.

NANA WAKES UP.

Nana: Ooh, that Advocaat – it doesn't half make me sleepy, Barbara.

Jim: Does it? Would you like another one, Norma?

Barbara: Oh, ey Antony, what time are you going to Emma's?

Antony: Well her mam said five for five-thirty, so I think that means about quarter-past.

Barbara: Ooh, ooh Antony, in't it funny you having to have two Christmas dinners.

Antony: Yeah s'all right really – well they're all vegetarians, so they're having a nut roast.

Jim: The tight gets. All that money and they won't fork out for a bit of turkey.

Nana: I can't believe they're having their Christmas dinner at night. Lay heavy on 'em, won't it.

Barbara: Yeah. Will you be staying late, Antony?

Antony: Yeah. Well, after they've had their dinner they always play charades, y'know, and parlour games 'n' that.

THEY ALL KILL THEMSELVES LAUGHING.

Jim: Parlour games!

Denise: Is their telly broke?

EVERYONE LAUGHS.

Jim: Parlour games my arse. Ey, tell you what you'd be good at, that's if they play it – hunt the Giro.

Barbara: Well I think they're right. We could do that – play some sort of a game. Ey Denise, do you remember that Christmas when we tried to play Rummy and your nana had two kings in her handbag.

Nana: I didn't know they were there, Barbara – but they did come in handy for that Royal Flush and I won £13 off Jim that night.

Barbara: Oh yes. Ey Jim, wasn't that the Christmas you didn't sleep?

Jim: Anyway, what do you want to go round there for, for all that bloody shite, when you could be here with us watching the bloody box? Parlour games my arse – they want to get out a bit more that lot.

Dave: What time are we going to my mam and dad's, Denise.

Denise: I don't really want to go Dave, why don't you go on your own?

Dave: Denise, me mam's doing a turkey buffet. There's only me and you going. If we don't turn up it'll only be me mam and dad – and me dad goes to bed early.

Denise: I don't really fancy it Dave. I feel a bit funny.

Jim: This is the one day of the year we all get together to watch the bloody television and look at the shite they put on. Well that's going for a burton. (JIM FLICKS THE REMOTE)

Nana: Oh, get off, Jim. I liked him, Noel Crinkly Bottom. You do whatever you like, you don't care about your family.

Jim: Oh, Crinkly Bottom my arse.

PAUSE.

Barbara: Did you like that turkey, Jim?

Jim: A little bit dry, weren't it, Barb?

Barbara: Did you, Mam?

Nana: I've never liked turkey, Barbara.

Barbara: Did you like it, Dave?

Dave: I could take it or leave it me, Barbara.

Barbara: Did you like it, Denise?

Denise: No, I didn't like it, there's no flavour.

Barbara: How about you, Antony?

Antony: I'm not bothered really, you know.

Barbara: Oh, I don't think I'll bother with getting a turkey next Christmas.

EVERYONE LOOKS HORRIFIED.

Jim: Why, what's the matter?

Dave: Barbara!

Denise: Mam! You've got to have a turkey at Christmas.

Jim: Bloody 'ell, Barb, don't be such a bloody killjoy.

Barbara: Well, you all made me get a Christmas pudding but none of you've had any. Ooh, I wonder how Cheryl's got on.

Mary's had to cook her a Weight Watchers Christmas dinner – y'know, low fat 'n' that.

Denise: Ah, has she?

Barbara: Yeah. Ooh. Mary said Cheryl's met a lovely new friend at Weight Watchers.

Denise: Has she?

Barbara: Yeah. A big fat girl from Hyde.

Denise: Aaah.

Jim: Oh, I like the sound of that, the big bride from Hyde.

Barbara: Let's all have a snowball? Don't snowballs make you feel Christmassy, ey?

Jim: Snowballs my arse. It's a bloody swizz this Christmas lark.

BARBARA MAKES THE SNOWBALLS ON THE DINING ROOM TABLE.

Nana: Denise, Denise, Denise, Denise. You know that book you bought for Cheryl, what's it about?

Denise: Oh, Feng Shui, Nana.

Nana: What's Feng Dooey?

Denise: Well, it's where you move everything round in your house, you know, to bring you happiness.

Nana: Oh.

Jim: I'd only have to move one thing in this house to make me happy.

Denise: Ey Nana, d'you know what Cheryl got me?

Nana: What?

Denise: A birthing tape.

Nana: What tape?

Denise: Well, she's put all me favourite songs on one tape, 'cause it said in the baby book, you know to relax you – y'know for when you're birthing.

Nana: She's a right big girl, is Cheryl, isn't she?

BARBARA RETURNS WITH FIVE SNOWBALLS AND HANDS THEM ALL OUT.

Barbara: Antony.

Antony: Cheers, Mam.

Barbara: Dave.

Dave: Thanks, Barbara.

Barbara: Here y'a.

Denise: Ta.

Barbara: Jim.

Jim: Ta, Barb.

Barbara: Here, Mam.

Nana: Ta, love. These always remind me of your dad, Barbara.

Jim: Here we go again.

Nana: He always used to make me a snowball. I always miss him more at Christmas you know – I don't know why.

Barbara: Aaah, Mam. Anyway, Happy Christmas everybody.

THEY ALL CLINK GLASSES.

Denise: Happy Christmas. Happy Christmas.

Barbara: Happy Christmas!

NANA DRINKS HER SNOWBALL DOWN IN ONE.

Jim: Bloody 'ell.

Barbara: Denise?

Denise: Yeah.

Barbara: Have you decided yet what you're going to do for the millennium?

Denise: Well, we talked about it for ages, didn't we Dave?

Dave: Umm.

Denise: In the end we decided we'd just come round here, really.

Barbara: Ah.

Dave: Um. Round here.

Barbara: Ah.

Denise: You still doing a buffet?

Barbara: Oh yeah. We've invited Mary and Joe and Cheryl.

Jim: Bloody 'ell. I hope you haven't invited Cheryl's bloody mate. There'll be no buffet left for us, if she gets at it. The big fat, lazy heifer.

Barbara: Mary's really looking forward to it, Joe's not really bothered. She said he can't get excited about the millennium.

Jim: Bloody 'ell, that's a surprise, isn't it. Millennium my arse. It's just another bloody swizz they've come up with to bloody rip me off, isn't it. Well I'm gonna treat it like any other New Year's Eve me. That's it. I'm gonna get totally bladdered and I'm doing nothing else, that's it, I'm doing nothing else. They can take it or leave it.

Denise: Who can, Dad?

Jim: Tony bloody Blair – and his show who've bloody organized it. It's all a bloody con to get more money out of me.

Nana: I'm stopping over on millennium night, aren't I, Barbara?

Barbara: Yeah.

Nana: I wouldn't want to miss it.

Barbara: No.

Jim: Why, what was the last one like, Norma?

Denise: Aah, it just kicked. D'you want a little feel, Dave?

Dave: Nah, you're all right.

DENISE LOOKS HURT.

Barbara: Oh. Could anyone eat a sandwich?

Dave: What's on it, Barbara?

Barbara: Well . . . turkey . . .

Dave: No thanks.

Barbara: The stuffing was a recipe from *This Morning* you know, Denise.

Denise: Oh.

Barbara: Mind you, I haven't got all the ingredients so I just mixed it with a bit of Paxo.

Denise: Oh.

Barbara: Ooh, you work so hard on that Christmas dinner, you're planning it for weeks – before you know it, it's all been eaten. What a waste.

Denise: Yeah. Have you finished the washing-up?

Barbara: No. Well I thought if your nana's not gonna be here tonight, I'd do it then.

Denise: Yeah.

Barbara: The kitchen's like Beirut, Denise.

Denise: Is it?

Barbara: Yeah.

Denise: Ey Nana, what time d'you have to be at Elsie's?

Nana: Oh well, I don't want to be late, Denise. Elsie goes to bed early you know with being housebound. It's the first time her daughter's ever left her at Christmas. South Africa they're going to. Cape Town. She's practically had everything out of Marks and Spencer, you know, for outfits for Cape Town.

Barbara: A lot of people are doing that now – going away for Christmas. I couldn't do it.

Jim: Well I bloody could. It's a complete bloody racket now Christmas, isn't it. It's a swizz, the bloody lot of it.

Barbara: Mam?

Nana: Umm?

Barbara: What did you get for Elsie in the end?

Nana: Ah well, you know that blue cardigan of mine? Well I never liked it on me – well, that.

Barbara: (TO THE OTHERS) I bought her that.

Jim: Ey Denise, it's bloody expensive to ring someone on one of them mobiles, so don't be expecting us to ring you on that.

Dave: They're for emergencies, them. Emergencies only.

Denise: I know, Dave. Oh God, you'd knock the good out of anything, you.

Barbara: Hey, David, Denise. It's Christmas Day! We're having our snowballs.

Antony: Ey, you know Emma's mam and dad?

All: Umm.

Antony: They've got a widescreen telly.

Jim: Have they, Lurch?

Antony: Yeah and it's got, eh, like panoramic sound. It's top.

Jim: Panoramic sound on it and they're playing all them stupid bloody parlour games. He must have money to burn him.

Barbara: Widescreen telly. Oh. D'you know, Denise, I'd love to watch your wedding video on a widescreen telly.

Denise: Yeah.

Nana: Yeah.

Barbara: Oh I would, I really, really would.

Denise: Ah. I'd love widescreen telly – it'd be absolutely brilliant.

Jim: You'd still see the same old shite on the bloody thing, but wider. What's the point in one of them?

Nana: What time is Dibley on? I do like that big funny girl – the one who dresses up as a vicar, you know.

Jim: Isn't it *Only Fools & Horses* on Barb? Where's the *Radio Times*?

Nana: Oh, I must have left it up in the toilet when I was trying earlier.

Jim: I had a Christmas log there myself, this morning, Dave. (RUBBING HIS HANDS) Oh you can't wack a good old Christmas log.

Denise: Dad! It's Christmas Day.

Jim: Christmas Day my arse.

PAUSE.

Nana: What time's dinner tomorrow, Barbara?

Barbara: About three o'clock, Mam.

Nana: I'll come at twelve o'clock just to be on the safe side.

Barbara: We're only going to be doing cold turkey and chips.

Nana: Lovely. No turkey for me, Barbara.

Barbara: Oh, I've got some sausage rolls there I could heat up. Now does anybody fancy a sausage roll? Jim?

Nana: No.

Jim: No.

Barbara: Ah. Denise, David?

Dave: No.

Barbara: Antony, have another Celebration, it is Christmas Day.

Antony: No y'all right, cheers, Mam.

Nana: Oh Barbara, I'd love a date. Where are they, Barbara?

BARBARA GETS THEM FROM THE COFFEE TABLE.

Barbara: Here.

Nana: 'Eat Me' dates! (SHE KILLS HERSELF LAUGHING) How do they think them up?

Antony: I think I'd best get off to Emma's.

Barbara: Antony, have you not got any presents to take round for 'em?

Antony: No. I gave Emma hers.

Barbara: Should I wrap some Roses up for you in a little bag? Look, if I take the wrappings out of here, you'd never know they'd been opened.

Antony: It's all right, I don't want to take them anything. It's all right. See you tomorrow, Nana. (HE KISSES HER) Oh, and cheers for that record token.

Nana: Oh all right, love.

Denise: Ey Antony, are you gonna tell Emma tonight that you love her?

ANTONY LOOKS VERY EMBARASSED.

Denise: You do love her. You love her. You do. You love her. He does love her.

ANTONY IS AT THE LIVING ROOM DOOR, ABOUT TO LEAVE.

Jim: Ey, Lurchio. (CHARADES STYLE) Film, book, stage play. Four words. First word (HE PATS HIS HEART), second word (HE POINTS TO HIS EYE), third word (HE MAKES A 'T' SIGN) and fourth word, sounds like (HE POINTS AT HIS ARSE): No? Love – on – the – dole. Are you having that, Dave?

Antony: See you later.

Nana: Bye bye, love.

Denise: See ya, Antony.

Barbara: Jim.

Jim: Well, I'm only giving him a bit of bloody practice for after the nut roast.

ANTONY GOES.

Nana: Ey Barbara, you know that stuff that Antony bought me from the Body Shop, don't ya? D'you know what it said on it, 'Not tested on animals'. What do you think?

Barbara: Why, what do you mean?

Nana: Well supposing some were to fall on a dog? I didn't say anything to Antony – wasn't his fault.

Barbara: No.

Denise: Hey Mam, this is the first time that our Antony's ever bought us any presents, innit?

Barbara: Yeah. Ey, she's good for him, that Emma isn't she?

Denise: Ah, he got me the Delia Smith cookery book.

Barbara: Aah.

Jim: Bloody 'ell, Dave – you might be getting coriander on the old, eh, Dairylea soon.

Barbara: Jim.

Jim: I know, bloody Christmas Day.

Denise: Ah, I love them gloves what Dad bought you, Mam.

Barbara: Yeah, well he didn't actually buy them for me. I bought them and I wrapped them – but he did write the tag.

Denise: Aaah.

PAUSE.

Nana: (TAKING DATE STONE OUT OF HER MOUTH) Barbara, what can I do with this stone?

Barbara: Oh here, Mam, put it in one of these sweetie wrappers.

Nana: Ta. (NANA GOES TO PUT THE WRAPPER BACK IN THE ROSES JAR)

Barbara: Oh, don't put it back in there, Mam!

Jim: I can't stop thinking about poor old Elsie on her own all day.

Nana: Oh Jim, you're right, I must go to her. (JIM SHOOTS DAVE A LOOK OF TRIUMPH) Will you give me a lift, Dave?

Dave: Course I will, Nana, yeah.

JIM COUGHS AND GESTURES TO GET NANA TO GO RIGHT AWAY.

Dave: Y'all right now then, Nana. I'll take you now.

Nana: All right then.

DAVE GOES INTO THE HALL.

Barbara: (GETTING UP TO GO TO THE KITCHEN) I've got some nice cold turkey and bit of stuffing for you to take to Elsie.

NANA STANDS UP AND GETS HER THINGS TOGETHER. DAVE (WEARING A CRASH HELMET) COMES BACK IN AND HANDS NANA HER COAT AND A CRASH HELMET.

Nana: Can I keep this hat, Barbara? I'd like to show it to Elsie, she'd like that, being housebound.

Barbara (OOV): D'you want to take her a hat, Mam?

Nana: Ooh, yes please, love, yeah.

Barbara: Well do you want to take her a cracker, Mam?

Nana: No, I don't think she'd be up to pulling it. She's very weak you know. I don't think she could stand the bang. Mind you I think she'd like one of them little toys. She's been a bit egg-bound lately, has Elsie. The bang might start the ball rolling.

Dave: Y'all right, Nana?

Jim: Egg-bound, housebound, not much hope for poor bloody Elsie is there?

NANA NOW WEARS HER COAT AND A CRASH HELMET. BARBARA HANDS HER A FOIL-COVERED PLATE AND HANDS DAVE AN M&S BAG.

Dave: Y'all right Nana?

Nana: Ta, love.

Barbara: Here y'a, Mam. Now all your presents are in there.

Nana: Oh thanks. Ey and thanks for getting them all from Marks's. I can take them back when they have a sale and get twice as much.

Denise: Bye, Nana. (KISSES HER)

Nana: Bye bye, love.

Denise: Thanks for the Boots voucher, Nana.

Nana: Oh, it's a pleasure love. See you tomorrow.

Denise: See ya.

Jim: Can't wait. Season's Greetings, Norma.

Nana: (AT THE DOOR) Oh Jim, I've marked off in the *Radio Times* what I want you to video for me. All right, love.

Dave: Won't be long.

Jim: You be careful swerving round them corners with Nana on the back, David – we don't want her falling off, do we.

BARBARA COMES BACK IN FROM THE HALL.

Barbara: In't Christmas Day a long day?

Denise: Yeah.

Barbara: I know it's the same as any other day – but oh, it does seem like a long day.

Denise: Yeah it does. Ey Mam, can you imagine me nana and Elsie in their hats?

Barbara: Aah.

Denise: They'll be asleep by seven.

Barbara: Aah. In't it lovely though when you get to that age, when all you have to think about is nodding off with somebody there.

Jim: Bugger off. She's only gone round there to save on her own gas bill.

Denise: Oh, guess what, I've got to go to the toilet.

DENISE LEAVES THE ROOM.

Jim: (OF DENISE) Bloody 'ell, it's Vanessa. Well I am as full as a bull's bum.

Barbara: Jim.

Jim: And tell you what Barb, don't bother heating up them sausage rolls – I'll just have a couple of light boiled eggs for my tea after all that rich food. Just do us a few soldiers. Cut the crusts off, will ya.

Barbara: Right. Oh Jim, I've got all that horrible washing-up to do.

Jim: Well, it won't do itself Barb. Tell Denise to bring the bloody *Radio Times* down, will ya.

BARBARA GOES TO THE FOOT OF THE STAIRS.

Barbara: Denise.

Denise (OOV): Mam! Will you come up!

IN THE LIVING ROOM JIM TRUMPS AND WAFTS IT AWAY, DISGUSTED BY THE SMELL.

BARBARA GOES INTO THE BATHROOM WHERE DENISE IS CRYING. WE ONLY SEE HER HEAD AND SHOULDERS, BUT SHE'S OBVIOUSLY SITTING ON THE TOILET.

Denise: Oh Mam, a load of water's came out. I think my waters have broken – and Dave's not even here.

Barbara: Oh Denise! Oh my God, Denise! Oh Denise. Oh love. Wait there – I'll go and ring Dave on the mobile.

Denise: Yeah. Yeah. Yeah. *I've* got the mobile.

Barbara: Oh God, Denise. Well I'll go and ring the hospital and I'll send your dad up. Jim!

Denise: Yeah, yeah.

Barbara: Jim!

Denise: Mam, don't leave me.

Barbara: Jim!

BARBARA RUNS DOWNSTAIRS INTO THE LIVING ROOM.

Barbara: Jim, get upstairs, our Denise's waters have broken.

Jim: What's broken, Barb?

Barbara: Her waters. Get upstairs and calm her down. She's all upset 'cause Dave's not here. Here, take her this, this birthing tape, go on, the tape's already in there. Come on now. (BARBARA HANDS JIM TAPE MACHINE AND TAPE)

Jim: Bloody 'ell Barb, what is it, the bloody *Dambusters* and Dave would have been here only for your bloody mother.

AS JIM GOES UP THE STAIRS HE HUMS THE THEME TO *THE DAMBUSTERS*.

Jim: Denise it's your dad, love.

Denise: Come in, Dad. Come in.

Jim: It's not too messy is it?

Denise: No. Come in.

HE GOES IN. DENISE IS SITTING ON THE EDGE OF THE BATH, DOUBLED OVER. JIM PUTS THE TOILET SEAT DOWN AND SITS ON IT, COMFORTING HIS SOBBING DAUGHTER.

Jim: You're all right. What's the matter?

Denise: I don't know, I can't even remember what I'm supposed to be doing out of me baby book. I'm supposed to be doing me breathing, but I can't even remember how to breathe.

Jim: Come on, you'll be all right. Here y'are, let's play your tape, eh? (CHARLOTTE CHURCH'S *'PIE JESU'* PLAYS IN THE BACKGROUND) Denise.

Denise: Yeah.

Jim: Are you definitely sure it wasn't just a great big piss, love.

Denise: No, I know it wasn't.

SILENCE AS *'PIE JESU'* PLAYS.

Denise: I don't know what I'm gonna do and Dave's gonna miss it and he's supposed to be helping me with me breathing and he's supposed to be counting them things – he's supposed to be counting 'em, them . . . things what I'm having. (REALLY SOBBING) Dad, I'm so scared and I don't even think I want the baby anymore. And I don't think Dave wants it either – he didn't even want to feel it kicking before and I bet ya he'll leave it all to me and I don't even know anything about babies.

Jim: You'll be all right – there's nothing to it.

Denise: What if the baby doesn't like me? What if I don't like the baby?

Jim: Of course you'll like it – you'll love it. I remember the first time when your mam, when your mam put you in my arms and I looked at you, oh God you were beautiful and I knew, I knew then, I'd do anything for you, anything for you and our Antony.

Denise: What if I'm not a good mum like me mam?

Jim: You will be a wonderful mother.

Denise: Dad, if Dave don't come back, will you come with me to the hospital?

Jim: Of course I will, I'll be right there outside. But your mam will be inside with you.

Denise: You promise you will, Dad? You will stay with me?

Jim: Of course I'll stay with you, I'll always be there for you. Always. Ey Denise, I'm gonna be a grandad.

BARBARA COMES IN.

Barbara: I've rang the hospital and they've told me to tell you to come in, so I've rang a taxi and it's on its way.

Jim: Bloody 'ell, Barb, it's double fare Christmas Day.

Barbara: Oh Jim! Come on now, lady, let's get you downstairs.

Jim: Come on, babe, let's go.

JIM AND BARBARA HELP DENISE DOWN.

Barbara: Here we go. Let me go first, love. Oh now, don't slip on this carpet, no shoes on your little feet. Are you all right?

Denise: Yeah.

Barbara: Are your hurting?

Denise: Yeah.

Barbara: It'll be over soon.

DENISE CRIES OUT IN PAIN.

Barbara: Sit down, love. Breathe, Denise. Breathe. Breathe. Good girl.

THE DOORBELL GOES.

Barbara: (GOING TO THE DOOR) Oh, let that be Dave, please let that be Dave. Oh Dave!

Dave: What's going on?

Barbara: It's all right, her waters have broken.

BARBARA AND DAVE STAND AT THE FOOT OF THE STAIRS.

Denise: Trust you not to be here when my waters broke. You're a right useless lump of shite.

Dave: I was taking your nana home.

Barbara: It's all right Dave. Ooh Denise, Denise, you might give birth on Christmas Day!

Jim: *Jesus.*

A TAXI BEEPS ITS HORN.

Barbara: Oh, oh, Jim, taxi. Oh, my ciggies.

BARBARA GOES INTO THE LIVING ROOM. DAVE OPENS THE FRONT DOOR TO SHOUT TO THE DRIVER.

Dave: Hang on a minute, pal.

Jim: Right. I'll just put my shoes on.

JIM FOLLOWS BARBARA INTO THE LIVING ROOM.

DAVE (STILL WEARING CRASH HELMET) SITS NEXT TO DENISE ON THE STAIRS.

Denise: I can't believe it, Dave, it's not due for three weeks. I hope it's gonna be all right.

Dave: It will. I love you, Denise.

DAVE GOES TO GIVE HER A HUG.

Denise: Oh Dave, your helmet you clown! (SHE HAS ANOTHER CONTRACTION) Mam! We need to go *now*. (DAVE GETS UP AND GOES) Dave, wait for me!

CUT TO LIVING ROOM.

Jim: (SWITCHING OFF ALL THE LIGHTS EXCEPT FOR THE CHRISTMAS TREE) We're switching these off, I'm not made of money.

Barbara: Oh Jim. Come on, your daughter's in agony. Get your coat on.

THE CAMERA STAYS IN THE LIVING ROOM AS JIM AND BARBARA GO OUT, CLOSING THE DOOR BEHIND THEM. WE SEE DAVE, DENISE, JIM AND BARBARA FILE PAST THE LIVING ROOM DOOR IN SILHOUETTE (BARBARA AND JIM STILL WEARING THEIR CHRISTMAS HATS).

END OF EPISODE 7.